PEEKing at Call-A.P.P.L.E.

APPLE PUGETSOUND PROGRAM LIBRARY EXCHANGE

1978

Compendium
of Magazine Articles

Produced by:

Brian Wiser & Bill Martens

 Apple PugetSound Program Library Exchange

Peeking at Call-A.P.P.L.E. 1978

Published by Apple Pugetsound Program Library Exchange (A.P.P.L.E.)
www.callapple.org

Paperback ISBN: 978-1-6781-6971-8
Hardback ISBN: 978-1-6781-7309-8

ACKNOWLEDGEMENTS

First and foremost, we would like to thank the original *Call-A.P.P.L.E.* magazine contributors from 1978: Darrell Aldrich, Ron Aldrich, John Backman, Dan Chapman, Robert Clardy, John Cook, John Covington, Jeffrey Finn, Val J. Golding, Alan Hill, Dick Hubert, Bob Huelsdonk, Gene Jackson, Neil Konzen, S.H. Lam, Steve Paulson, Dana Redington, Michael Scott, Dick Sedgewick, Michael Thyng, Roger Wagner, Michael Weinstock, Randy Wigginton, Don Williams, and Steve Wozniak.

Thanks to everyone who joined the A.P.P.L.E. user group, read *Call-A.P.P.L.E.* magazine, made contributions, and supported our endeavors.

The Cover and Book were designed by Brian Wiser.

PRODUCTION

Brian Wiser → Design, Layout, Editing
Bill Martens → Scanning, Production

DISCLAIMER

About the Producers

Val J. Golding

Val J. Golding founded Apple Pugetsound Program Library Exchange (A.P.P.L.E.) in 1978 with the help of Mike Thyng and Bob Huelsdonk at the suggestion of Max Cook, a manager at the ComputerLand where Val bought his Apple II. A.P.P.L.E. was one of the first official Apple User Groups in the United States

During his usual trip to the ComputerLand store, Val met another Apple II owner, Bob Huelsdonk. Val and Bob talked for some length of time with Max Cook and decided that as information about the Apple II was scant, that they should start an Apple User Group.

Val created a one page notice of a meeting and distributed it to all of the Apple II owners who were on the customer lists of ComputerLand, Empire Electronics, and Omega Stereo. The date that was set for this meeting was the 16th of February, 1978.

At that first meeting, about 20 people attended with 12 of them joining the group after the meeting. From this humble beginning, the group incorporated in 1979 as a non-profit organization and promptly grew beyond all expectations reaching 5,000 members by 1980, 12,000 by 1981, and peaking at almost 50,000 global members by 1985.

Val also wrote for *Softdisk*, On-three and other technology magazines over the years primarily making his mark in the early years of Apple computing.

As the founder, Val was instrumental in guiding the company to the position it is in now. Val was the Managing Editor of *Call-A.P.P.L.E.* magazine and also served as the chairman of the board of directors.

His wife and daughters were a big part of documenting his stories about his hobby of Cable Cars, and he was the editor of a highly acclaimed newsletter for his daughter's school. He passed away at age 77 on July 2, 2008 after a long battle with cancer.

Brian Wiser

Brian Wiser is a producer of books, films, games, and events, as well as a long-time consultant, enthusiast and historian of Apple, the Apple II and Macintosh. Steve Wozniak and Steve Jobs, as well as *Creative Computing*, *Nibble*, *InCider*, and *A+* magazines were early influences.

Brian designed, edited, and co-produced dozens of books including: *Nibble Viewpoints: Business Insights From The Computing Revolution*, *Cyber Jack: The Adventures of Robert Clardy and Synergistic Software*, *Synergistic Software: The Early Games*, *The Colossal Computer Cartoon Book: Enhanced Edition*, *All About Applesoft: Enhanced Edition*, *Graphically Speaking: Enhanced Edition*, *What's Where in the Apple: Enhanced Edition*, and *The WOZPAK: Special Edition* – an important Apple II historical book with Steve Wozniak's restored original, technical handwritten notes. Brian is also the author of *The Etch-a-Sketch and Other Fun Programs*.

He passionately preserves and archives all facets of Apple's history, and noteworthy companies such as Beagle Bros and Applied Engineering, featured on AppleArchives.com. His writing, interviews and books are featured on the technology news site CallApple.org and in *Call-A.P.P.L.E.* magazine that he co-produces as an A.P.P.L.E. board member. Brian also co-produced the retro iOS game *Structris*.

In 2005, Brian was cast as an extra in Joss Whedon's movie *Serenity*, leading him to being a producer and director for the documentary film *Done The Impossible: The Fans' Tale of Firefly & Serenity*. He brought some of the *Firefly* cast aboard his Browncoat Cruise and recruited several of the *Firefly* cast to appear in a film for charity. Throughout these experiences, he develops close personal relationships with many actors, authors, and computer industry luminaries. Brian speaks about his adventures to large audiences at conventions around the country.

Bill Martens

Bill Martens is a systems engineer specializing in office infrastructures and has been programming since 1976. The DEC PDP 11/40 with ASR-33 Teletypes and CRT's were his first computing platforms with his first forays in the Apple world coming with the Apple II computer.

Influences in Bill's computing life came from *Byte* magazine, *Creative Computing* magazine, and *Call-A.P.P.L.E.* magazine as well as his mentors Samuel Perkins, Don Williams, Joff Morgan, and Mike Christensen.

Bill is the author of *ApPilot/W1*, *Beyond Quest*, *The Anatomy of an EAMON*, and multiple EAMon adventure games, as well as a co-producer of many books including *What's Where in the Apple: Enhanced Edition*, *The WOZPAK: Special Edition*, *Nibble Viewpoints: Business Insights From The Computing Revolution*, and co-programmer for the iOS version of the retro game *Structris*. He has written many articles which have appeared in user group newsletters and magazines such as *Call-A.P.P.L.E.*.

Bill worked for Apple Pugetsound Program Library Exchange (A.P.P.L.E.) under Val Golding and Dick Hubert as a data manager and programmer in the 1980s, and is the current president of the A.P.P.L.E. user group established in 1978. He reorganized A.P.P.L.E. and restarted *Call-A.P.P.L.E.* magazine in 2002. He is the production editor for the A.P.P.L.E. website CallApple.org, writes science fiction novels in his spare time, and is a retired semi-pro football player.

CONTENTS

Basically Speaking

Color Graphics

Disk

Printing

Miscellaneous

INTRODUCTION

These are the first words I've written for Call-Apple not in the third person, a form I've become acustomed to over the years. The occasion, if you care to express it as such, is the first anniversary of Call-Apple, and the publication of PEEKing at Call-Apple.

The Apple Pugetsound Program Library Exchange was "born" at the Federal Way, Washington store of Computerland in February of 1978. Its birth was not spectacular, nor was it even noted in the daily journals, and it was only one of many groups to be spawned from the popularity of the Apple II Computer.

Now, almost a year later, A.P.P.L.E. has become an international organization, with members in most states and more than seven foreign countries and a roster approaching 500 members. It was never intended to be such, nor had I any premonition that it would achieve the recognition that it has to day.

My Apple II was purchased in late December of 1977. I was a pure novice, never having had hands-on experience with any kind of computer. Early the next January I was in the Computerland store again and had the occasion to talk with and meet Bob Huelsdonk who has had some prior experience with programming. As we were exchanging ideas and information, Bob suggested that perhaps we might form a group that would be able to more widely disseminate information, and perhaps exchange programs between members.

Max Cook, the owner of Computerland, at this point offered to donate the use of his store as a meeting place, which we accepted on the spot. The February Call-Apple, if indeed there was one, was primarily a notice of the initial meeting, along with a couple of news and gossip items. I ran 50 copies of a single page on my office photocopy machine, and mailed them to assorted individuals who might be interested.

The March issue of our little newletter had doubled in size and circulation (both sides of one page and 100 copies printed) and it also aquired a name: Call-Apple. The rest is history, so to speak. Each issue grew in pages, circulation and quality of editorial content. Call-Apple was first composed on an antique IBM Executive, then with my Apple and Integral Data printer and finally, as it became more and more time-consuming, by a commerical typesetter.

By July, the circulation had risen to the point where it took many hours on the office copy machine and therefore the August issue went to a commercial printer for the first time. By fall, I had reprinted several back issues on a number of occasions, and judging by the stream of requests, the end is not in sight.

I felt, and apparently many of Call-Apple's readers agreed, that there was much valuable information in these past issues, and consequently I would reprint from time to time, some of the more valuable information such as the Integer and Applesoft token charts, for the benefit of the newer members. But even this is poor use of magazine space, when there is newer and unpublished material available.

Michael Weinstock and George Beasley in Florida called me one day to suggest a reprint, in bound volume form, of the 1978 Call-Apples. I recall I said something to the effect that it was a good idea, but that there was no time available to undertake a project of this nature, whereupon Michael and George volunteered to handle the project from Florida.

PEEKing at CALL-A.P.P.L.E., then is their stepchild. It has been edited and organized into sections dealing with specific subjects, Integer Basic, Applesoft, Disk, hardware, etc. They have put a great deal of effort into this project, and I believe it will become a valuable reference work and one that every Apple owner, member or not, will want to own.

PEEKing at CALL-A.P.P.L.E., Volume I is therefore dedicated to Michael Weinstock and George Beasley who brought it to fruition.

                              Val J. Golding
                              President
                              Apple Pugetsound Program
                              Library Exchange

POKEs From The Editor

Well, it's finally here. After months of planning and
cross-country coordination, we finally got this edition to
the printer. Val Golding, the A.P.P.L.E. hard-working,
industrious, benevolent club president (do I get my raise
now, boss?) and I have made 1978 a profitable year for
Ma Bell: Val lives in Washington, while I live in Florida.

A few words of explaination are in order. We have
reproduced most of the 1978 Call-A.P.P.L.E. articles with
corrections (if any) incorporated. All the old ads have
beed deleted. Rather than leave blanks, we have added
APPLE II information gleaned from other sources. These
items are flagged by a "*". Each section is printed in a
separate color to facilitate locating articles of interest.

We sincerely hope that you will enjoy your edition of
PEEKing at Call-A.P.P.L.E. There is a wealth of information here. If you have any articles of interest,
fascinating facts, or programs you would like to share
with others, please contact Val at the club address. We
exist to support you. If you would like to join A.P.P.L.E.
and receive our monthly publication, an Apple-cation
blank is in the back of the book.

Happy programming!

MICHAEL D. WEINSTOCK
GEORGE C. BEASLEY, JR.

Call -A. P. P. L. E.

APPLE PUGETSOUND PROGRAM LIBRARY EXCHANGE

General

A <u>GENERAL</u> SECTION FROM THE BOTTOM OF THE

APPLE BARREL

APPLE HISTORY

APPLE REVIEWS

APPLE SOURCE

and

SOME INTERESTING LETTERS

and MORE!

Dear Sirs:

Being the wife of an Apple computer nut, I felt other women in my predicament would appreciate this little tribute. I would appreciate it if you would publish it in your next monthly newsletter.

"For the Apple Widows"

Attention ladies ...
I'm in distress!!
My eyelids are twitching
My head's all a mess.

I married into
A strange family
Where life is comprised
Of monitors and keys.

With PEEK and POKE
and LOAD and RUN
Any sabotage
Is a job well done!

From Qubic, Artillery,
Pong and Star Wars,
My brain has just about
Run it's course!!

I know computers
Are entertaining and neat,
But when your husband
Forgets to breathe and eat???

I suppose, I suppose I could
Refuse to fight
Just wash the dishes
And accept my plight.

Would someone, somehow,
Somewhere please
Help me control this
New disease?

If you have an idea
That's unusually great
I'll be in EMMANUEL
Psych. Ward, Rm. 208.

Cindy Rogers
934 N.E. 73rd
Portland, OR 97213

WE'RE SURE you are not alone!

A BRIEF HISTORY of APPLE

by Michael M. Scott, President

Presented at the September 12, 1978 meeting of A.P.P.L.E

Apple was started two and a half years ago by two gentlemen, Steve Jobs and Steve Wozniak who met at the "home brew" computer club at the Stanford accelerator. there, they got together and put into manufacture the Apple 1, which was a single-board, black and white -basically a fancy monitor- that worked with a TV set. A year later, they were joined by three other gentlemen, that's myself (Mike Scott), Mike Markulla and Rod Holte, and formed Apple Computer, inc. and went about the business of making the Apple II.

To give a little background on the five of us: Jobs is from Atari and, in fact, was the inventor of the "breakout" game that you see around a lot. Wozniak was in the advanced calculator group at h-p, and tried to interest h-p in doing a home computer, but they weren't interested, so he started working in his garage. Rod Holt was previously with Hickock as head of engineering and more recently at Atari and he did Apple's switching power supply and does the analog circuits and the rest of the support engineering.

Mike Markulla was originally with Hughes aircraft and most recently had been with Intel as head of marketing and had been retired from there about a year and a half when he came to us, and I most recently was director of hybrids and transducers at National Semiconductor. So we have a mixed crew and have expanded on it.

So we had five. February, a year and a half ago, we introduced the Apple II at the first West Coast Computer Faire on April 5th, 1977. We shipped the first Apple II last June -sorry- June a year ago. This last June was out first million dollar sales month, and where we thought business was excellent and getting better, in the last three or four months it's improved even further.

The company has sought and obtained outside financing. We have a very small percentage of the company; the stock has been sold to private firms or individuals. In particular, we did this to establish more credence with banks and other people that we could obtain financing from, and also to obtain outside advice on how not to get into trouble. The principal outside contributors are: Benrock, which is part of the Rockefeller Foundation. They're the country's oldest capital venture firm. The other group is Capital Management, and they were the firm that originally financed Atari and arranged for the Warner buy-out of Atari And Capital now owns ten percent of Warner.

We have a couple of private gentlemen; one is Art Brock who is known in the San Francisco area for his financing of such companies as Intel, Intercil, Fairchild and Quantel. It's not been made public yet, but joining our board as of a week and a half ago is an Apple freak who has one of the earliest Apples, with one at his home and one at his office. His name is Henry Singleton. He does not sit on any outside boards, but has given us the honor of joining Apple's Board of Directors. For those who don't know, eighteen years ago, with fifteen hundred dollars cash, he started a little company called Teledyne, Inc., and he is still Chairman of the Board, partially retired, the head of a 2.5 billion-dollar-a-year company. He doesn't program in Basic or any of the other languages; he programs in machine language only. He's one of the five people we know who uses the internal floating point package to do financial analyses on the Apple. That's what he does at work for relaxation. And now he's working on a chess program which finds any three moves in a little less than a second right now. So we're looking forward to his participation and advice.

The company grew then, from the original five people; we currently, as of the last count, have 74 direct employees at the main Cupertino plant. We have 340 authorized stores right now and are sold internationally in almost every single country in the world, including throughout Europe, South America and the far east. International sales represent about 25% of our sales right now. We have indirectly working for Apple Computer then, about another 100 people through sub-contractors. We specialize at the main plant; what we do is buy all the material. We then kit it, like Heathkit. We kit it out to sub-contractors who do the actual assembly of the PC board, and the insertion and the soldering. Then it returns to Apple where we do a board level test, a 24 hour burn in, and a final systems test.

So we try to keep down the amount of square footage that we need for expansion. One and a half years ago, we had 800 square feet. In the next six months we picked up another 3000. Last February, only six months ago, we swore it was enough space for 18 months when we moved into our new facility that was 21,000 square feet. A month ago we picked up another 5000, and we are next week picking up another 40,000 right in the same area. And that's keeping down what we do in the plant.

What we have inside now in the way of groups, is in the marketing group. We now have a fairly complex marketing group. We have an applications engineer full time in marketing; we're adding one to the engineering group to answer questions. We still encourage the local clubs or the local dealers to filter it, or that the questions that come in, come in in writing, so we can combine them and put them out in the Contact newsletter. We have hired a full time service manager who will set up a separate service department.

We have hired a full time publications group which consists of eleven people, partially made up of five text editors, and we still have not been able to keep up with the rate at which we need to document to put out a good manual. I'll give you two examples: one is the disk manual, which is atrocious, and we hope to have a revision in a couple of months; but it takes time to do it, and do it right. Applesoft II: hopefully the final revision is in print; this is a shrunk version, and it will be the same size as the Basic programming manual. It is not tutorial, but it goes exactly into the syntax of how the current released version of Applesoft II works.

Separate from the publications department, we have an inside group of ten people doing programming that's working on dedicated, user-related (DowJones types) and other types. Besides the user-contributor group, we now have under contract five different outside groups doing software packages for us. We will in the future introduce packages for small business that will be Apple supported as opposed to user-supported, where we say "you can have copies, but don't call us if there's a bug".

We're also looking at having an educational package. We have a well-known educational group doing some languages that are used for the high schools and colleges in teaching, to go on the Apple. Within the last three or four weeks we have added –he's not officially on our board till the 25th– a gentleman named Lloyd Martin from H-P who will head our applications software group. He, for your information, is the one that has headed the development software group at HP and done the applications package for the HP-45 series of programmable calculators.

We've added two additional gentlemen inside Apple, one is Bill Thomas, who is starting the 18th. Bill is one of the original founders of Four-Phase. Did their software for their systems; did their Cobol compiler. He's joining us as manager of our systems software group. The other gentleman was head of the design team at Motorola on the 6800 microprocessor; he did the 6502 design at Mostech, and is the architect of the patent. That's Chuck Pettle, and Chuck joined us yesterday from Commodore.

I'd say as a company a lot of people said "well, are you going to bring out a different product each year?". I think we've already shown that we don't have that intention. We certainly over the next couple of years will introduce other mainframe products. We think of the Apple II as being useful to the user for five to ten years and plan to continue supporting it with additional periferals and expanding the software that will run on the system. The more recent periferals out include the disk, which nobody can get enough of. This illustrates a problem we have; we have established a user base, so whenever we announce <a new product> we are immediately sold out for 8 to 12 weeks. A short example: we announced the communications card and put 500 in stock because marketing said that would be enough, and we sold out in two weeks, then we started the production cycle again.

The Applesoft ROM card: we made an initial pre-production run of 2500, and also sold those out in less than two weeks. The disk we knew we were going to be in trouble on. We are the largest supplier of mini-drives in the world now, because we do business with Shugart, who makes 90% of the drives. We're their largest customer now and have been for four months. So those who haven't got theirs yet, be patient; current lead time is about 6 to 8 weeks on new orders. Those stores who had early orders in were supplied first on the disk drive.

There are newer periferals coming; a high speed serial card is in manufacturing and should be ready in 4 to 5 weeks. As soon as the manual is ready -since the manual is most of it- we will announce what we call the "Programmer's Aid" ROM, which is in stock now except for the manual, which will be ready in about four weeks. It plugs into slot B0 on the main Apple board and gives such things as <Gary> Shannon's tone routines in firmware, hires routines in firmware, a tape verify routine and some other utility routines that are crammed on that 2K of code. We're interested in your input. You will be receiving in the mail, those of you who have your warranty cards in in the next couple of months, a questionaire to help us decide on what new periferals, or new software, or what new generation products we should look at, and we'd appreciate your inputs on it. For those of you who know people who don't have their warranty cards in, please encourage them to fill one out and send it in. That is how we key the mailing of the Contact users group and any updates that we have.

RESTRICTED PROGRAMS

Certain copyrighted programs carry restrictions in the REMarks lines or elsewhere that they may not be duplicated, reproduced or sold, and for good reason. We would like to discourage from the outset, the practice of duplicating, either on tape or by printouts, of any program that has such a restriction. A recent article indicated that the cost per Basic line of debugged software has risen to an all time high of $8. Selling these programs to the consumer, either directly, or through magazine and book publication, is the only way of recovering those costs. We will not knowingly tolerate, or be a party to such practices.

DON'T CALL APPLE, CALL -APPLE !

As we have mentioned in the past, we have received only the greatest support in the world from Apple Computer, Inc. There was a time when Apple owners were a very small minority among personal computer users. Not so now, when Apple is outselling all others. We imagine that in that dim distant past, Phil or Woz or Randy probably enjoyed an occasional phone call from a user. Presently, however, we suspect that those good people may be rather plagued by calls. After all, they certainly are expected to do some programming or whatever. Anyway, what we are obtusely pointing to is before you call Apple, call -Apple, or talk to your area dealer. There are now Apple user groups in many parts of the country, and most all we know usually talk to Apple frequently. So why not first route your calls to the clubs or dealers. Many problems and questions we feel can be resolve at the local level. The Call -Apple "Hot Line" is (206) 932-6588. Try it, you'll like it!

APPLE BOXES

We have had a number of inquiries as to what the Apple Box is. Essentially, it is just a simple interface between the cassette recorder and the telephone line. When the transmit/receive switch is in either on position, the phone line is held open and you may send from recorder to recorder. Under certain circumstances you may also send directly to or from the Apple, if the recorder involved has no ground loops.

Production is way, way behind on this item and back orders we hope to ship by February 1st.

EDITORIAL by Val J. Golding

Is the ugly head of price wars and cutthroat sales about to raise itself? We sincerely hope not. These are bargains in which no one gains. If a dealer can move enough units in a given period of time, he can make money, even with a profit margin as low as 10%. But in order to do this, he must also cut overhead.

This is usually accomplished through reductions in sales staff and services to customers. Needless to say, it is the customers who stand to lose the most. Service costs money. And the product is a loser, too. We have seen good audio products go down the drain with uncontrolled price cutting. And this is not too say a dealer can't wheel and deal a bit, but within limits!

REVIEW by Val Golding

APPLESOFT II Extended Precision Floating Point Basic. $20 from Apple dealers or direct from Apple Computer, 10260 Bandley Drive, Cuptertino, CA 95014. Supplied free with new 16-48K Apples. A ROM version is expected to be released about July 1st for $99.

One's first impression might be that charging for this updated version of Applesoft is unfair, which was our snap judgement. However, consideration must be given to other facts, the first being that Apple Computer has spent a small fortune in development costs and programming expense, and through the sale of the cassette tapes is attempting to recoupt only a small portion of that expense. Secondly, Applesoft II is so much modified from the original that it should properly be considered as a new Basic, rather than a modification. And on this basis, a search through magazine ads reveals that many computer owners, Altair, Imsai, etc., pay hundreds of dollars for a good extended Basic, still not a "rip-off" price, once again taking development costs into account.

Despite it's superior string handling capabilities, we have avoided Applesoft I for a number of reasons, including the many format differences from the faster running Integer Basic, and the lack of immediate error messages, owing to the manner in which the two respective Basics are compiled. Many of these items, minor in themselves, such as the use of a hyphen instead of a comma in the LIST command, have been rectified. In contrast, the listing format has also been revised, with the consequence that, like Integer Basic, one must now utilize the POKE 33,33 routine to avoid tracing over the gaps in long print statements. In addition, it is also necessary to backspace with escape "B" to copy a line number. Apple says this will not be changed. Mores the pity.

Applesoft II contains over 35 new or modified commands, in addition to most of the originals. Whenever possible, command names have been changed to match those of Integer Basic, a much needed change. The renamed commands are: GR, PLOT, COLOR=, HLIN, VLIN, TEXT, CALL and HTAB. The new commands include FLASH, INVERSE and NORMAL; TRACE and NOTRACE; STORE and RECALL; ONERRGOTO and RESUME; HOME; POP; SPEED. The latter intrigues us as it provides a means for the first time to control the output speed to either printer or screen, and we have found it most useful in listing programs. We are happy to see the powerful TRACE debug command added, but regret that no room was left to include the handy DSP and AUTO. But then, there is room for only 128 such tokens. (See the Applesoft II token chart elsewhere in this issue.) In addition to the foregoing, there are about a dozen commands committed to the handling of High Resolution graphics, available for the first time in Applesoft.

Apple has indicated that the random number generator has now been repaired, and that math accuracy has been improved. As is the case with earlier Apple documentation, the eight pages that come with the cassette as a supplement to the Applesoft manual leave something to be desired. A case in point. In our first attempt to use the Applesoft II HIRES routines, we struggled through the list of commands, noted one error and one ommission and finally managed to draw some lines on the screen. The colors are still a mystery to us, behaving quite differently in vertical and horizontal modes.

Were this to be used with some of the earlier component-based microcomputer systems we would state that the documentation was adequate, since for the most part users are assumed to have some background in data processing. Such is not the case with Apple II, the forerunner of a new generation of "plug-in-and-run" micro-computers. Hopefully, by the time the ROM version is released, Apple will have completely revised the Applesoft manual.

In all fairness, we must also offer our opinion that in the final analysis, Applesoft II will come to be known as one of the most versatile and powerful extended Basics available, and we suspect that we will personally be making a great deal more use of "ASII" than we did of it's predecessor.

LIBRARY PAK 1A owners: There is a partial dropout in program No. 8 (Color Game Pak) in early copies. Try loading at a higher volume setting. If this does not work, let us know and we will replace. Also early copies of Basic Tutorial.

EDITORIAL   by Val J. Golding

A problem that arises in any such organization as A.P.P.L.E. is that of "Bootlegging programs." We have a number of programs in our personal library which we have purchased from a software vendor, and when a friend says: "Gosh, that's a neat program..will you run me a copy off?", we have to decline. Not because we don't want to pass the program on, but because we happen to believe that the author/owner of software is entitled to remuneration for his efforts, which is not possible when a program is freely duplicated and passed from person to person. This is why the author has placed a copyright line somewhere in the program.

Our club policy is oriented towards providing the membership with a maximum amount of software at the lowest possible cost, but this does not include adding saleable programs to our library unless we can make an agreement with a vendor to distribute his program, which we have done in some cases.

We would like to discourage from the outset the practice of duplicating, either on tape or printout, programs that carry copyright restrictions. We will not knowingly tolerate, or be a party to such practices.

REVIEWS   by Val Golding

At the top of the list is Apple Computer's new Basic programming manual. This falls just short of being a masterpiece. It is well written and easy to understand, even for a novice like this writer and is printed in a small, easy to handle spiral binding. It starts by introducing simple Basic commands in program format and in each simple program, goes on to bring a new command into action. If you have not yet recieved your copy, ask your dealer.

The April-May issue of MICRO, the 6502 journal, reached our desk just in time to be included in this review. Here is a Magazine that is a must for the serious Apple II owner. Every issue to date has had material on Apple II, and this is no exception with an Applesoft Variables chart and an Apple II Programmers guide, an update on a prior article about interfacing a printer to Apple, and comments about the clocking system used by the μp. The guide contains many good hints and routines that are not to be found in the owners manual.

Other articles cover a morse code program for KIM-1, other KIM-1 and PET related stories, words on a standard 6502 Assembly Syntax, Micro's software catalogue and Part III of a 6502 bibliography. It is published bimonthly by "the Computerist' at 8 Fourth Lane, S. Chelmsford, Ma. 01824, $6.00 per year. Run, don't walk!

Last, but certainly not least, is Dr. Dobbs Journal of Computer Calisthenics & Orthodontia, published 10 times per year by Peoples Computer Company, Box E, Menlo Park, Ca. 94025, at $12.00 per annum. Unlike Micro, Dr. Dobbs is not 6502-oriented. However, it appears that the software section each issue has programs for the four popular chips, 6502, 6800, Z-80 and 8080. In addition, it would appear that about every other issue has material pertinent to Apple II., this one being no exception, with a Renum/Append routine being featured. This journal does not accept paid commercial advertising, on the premise of "keeping us honest, while pursuing the role of consumer advocate. We agree,

APPLE SOURCE

Transcribed by Mike Thyng

The following transcription is an approximation of the question and answer session held at the September meeting at Computerland of Bellevue where Apple President Mike Scott and Randy Wigginton addressed members. Many people were too far away to be clearly recorded. Other times, someone would cough or shuffle when a key word was spoken by a distant or soft speaker. So I have tried to relate as accurately as possible the intent of the questions and remarks by both sides.

In this portion Q. = club members. A. = Mike Scott A. The Apple disk drives are not intended to be used with other computers. The APPLE hardware was designed to be integral and interactive within the APPLE. The APPLE disks are soft sectored. The drive is not a standard Shugart 400 drive. The Shugart Standard Analog Board has 23 IC's; APPLE had 4. The S-100 controller card has 30 IC's - the APPLE has 8. APPLE accomplished substantial savings by tying the design together of the software firmware, and hardware. You can cut a notch in the other side and use both sides of the diskettes.

2A is the identifier of the most current version of APPLESOFT II. Disk was released with only the right version of APPLESOFT. The ROM card is gospel.

Q. You changed the definition of LOMEM in APPLESOFT. Is there any way to get the equivalent Integer Basic LOMEM from APPLESOFT?

A. You mean so it doesn't use memory belowa certain point? Yes, there is. Do a POKE of 103, 104. This is the base address of your APPLESOFT program. If you have a ROM card and disk and your programs are saved onto the disk, with the RAM version you have to do a call. What's happening is that we have to relocate all the pointers down for the ROM Card and back up for the RAM version. So if you adjust 103, 104 then you're going to have to do those calls. From RAM to ROM call 54514. From ROM to RAM (in memory) call 3314. Loading from tape you never have those problems. It does it all automatically. See Val's write up about the ampersand

Q. I've had problems initializing disks from my master create program. A. Easiest solution is to move the disk card from slot 6 to slot 7. When the new version of the DOS comes out, we'll have that corrected. We wanted to standardize the slots and leave slot 7 open for a possible video interface card if and when we ever do an 80 character or some other video interface. When APPLE wrote the DOS for the European Market the boards were in slot 7. Then shortly before USA release they were switched from slot 7 to slot 6. Not all the software routines were changed back. There's a new manual being printed that will explain much more about your APPLE. Expected distribution is in OCTOBER. 180 pages long; detail about how exactly APPLESOFT works.

Q. Is PASCAL software being developed for the APPLE? A. Not by APPLE but by a company in San Diego. Q. What languages are you planning to introduce? A. I'm not at liberty to say which, but APPLE has contracted with outside software suppliers to provide a second and a third generation language. Q. When will we get a real time clock? A. We've worked on it some. The problem now is the high cost. It's on our list of things to do. Q. How many APPLEs are there? A. Everybody wants to know. It's a well kept secret. Many, many thousands. A. We allocate product on a first order in - first order out. If we don't have enough to fill all the orders fully then we allocated a percentage to each order so everybody gets some.

THE NEXT PORTION IS BEING FIELDED BY RANDY WIGGINGTON. RANDY WRITES SYSTEMS SOFTWARE DID APPLESOFT II AND WROTE PART OF THE DOS.

Memory allocation starts at hex location 800 for the ROM cards. The variables are located immediately after the program. First it's simple variables, then array variables. String arrays have pointers. A$ = "HELLO" has pointers that point inside the program. A$ = B$ then B$ points to A$. Strings are allocated memory from high memory down. If you set A$ = something and B$ = Something, and C$ = something, and then change it, you are leaving blanks. These blanks stay there until you run the program; then the program shifts things around. This explains why a large program may take many minutes to run. It has a lot of number crunching to do. I gave Val Golding about 2 inches of documentation and miscellaneous things.

You could have 6 colors in HIRES: HCOLOR = 0, 4 black 3, 7 white then 1, 2, 5, 6 could be four other colors but unnamed because the way you adjust the TV set would alter the colors. Future versions of DOS call for it to be about 3K rather than the present 11K. Val has the RWTS routines that let you use the disk directly. All the new stuff will be on DOS. The Interface to disk requires that when you write to disk you input the command number, specify whether you want to format the disk, read or write the track and sector data.

Q. You can't write a "to disk" can you? A. Anytime you want to get a "to the disk, write CHR$(n), where n is the numerical decimal equivalent of the character." A. The new manual will have stuff about how to create your own save tape. A Macro assembler will be coming out ... Q. I've got a file on my disk that was written with an illegal character and now I want to delete it. A. Initialize the disk. Only way presently. Q. What about a copy? A. That would only transfer the bogus data to the new disk. Q. I did an open, a write and a CATALOG and the CATALOG cancelled out the write. I wanted to get a copy of the CATALOG out on a text file so I could bring it in later and .... A. Whenever you go into write mode, anytime you print a control D or try to do an input you'll move out of write mode. Basically there is no way presently that you can get your catalog written out. The Catalog is located on disk at tracks 17 & 18. APPLE has spent many hours trying to find ways to neatly read the Catalog but so far no success. Checkbook II has a way to do this, but it's not elegant.

Many questions about the disk format. Data written out is in ASCII Mode. When or if you Print A, B the data would go out as it would look on the display screen. But, and this is a big one, you could not read back that A, B as A, B. The disk sees that as all one variable. Don't panic. The solution is to PRINT A: PRINT B. What's required is to get the variables seperated by a carriage return symbol. Individual Prints do that. Q. I have trouble converting programs from magazines (written for other computer's BASIC's) to programs for my APPLE. A. We're working on it.

Q. How often will CONTACT come out? A. We're working on every two months, but not yet. In the future, perhaps every month. Q. Does the APPLE see A and shift A as the same character? A. Unmodified, yes. I have given Val information on lower case. If you add a wire to the keyboard then lower case characters will display as reverse video. Q. I can't get the other square bracket to print. A. Try PRINT CHRS (154). Or something close to 154. Q. Does the disk store PR # someplace? A. You mean it's own character out switches? Q. Where are they? A. Up in High Memory somewhere.

My printer is hooked up to the Communications interface card and when I use a comma, it doesn't seem to recognize it. A. When we hit a comma, we change the cursor horizontal directly in memory. On the printer card we check to see if the cursor horizontal jumps by more than 1. If it does, it puts in the extra spaces. The Communications Card does not do that. I suggest you TAB or use the Space command. Q. When I try to print out 3 strings AS, BS, CS and use commas, depending on the length of the second string, I may print on line 1 or line 2 ... what gives? A. Plain and simple, I made an error. I meant to check 33 instead of 23. Q. How do you determine how much space you have left on your disk? A. You know those Numbers just ahead of the program names in the CATALOG? Well those are completely random. Actually there isn't a way.

Q. My APPLE's DOS won't let me read or write above 256. What gives? A. You have an earlier version. Your club has the patch. Q. HTAB doesn't work above 40 characters on my printer. A. POKE 36, value will do it for you. Q. Do we have indirect addressing in BASIC? A. No. A. DOS documentation and a revised version of the DOS will be coming out.

A. When you have problems, suggestions, or comments ... write them in - don't call. We can't be effective by phone. Q. I have a mix of 16K and 4K chips ...A. DOS can handle it. Q. Does the Communication Interface card handle the IBM BAUD rate of 134? A. I think that is one on the standard selections ... if not, the manual that came with it can tell you how to set it to that rate. A. There is a new high speed serial interface card coming out - up to 19K baud. Switch and software selectable. Q. I have an idea for a change to the case of the APPLE II. A. We're not likely to make any changes to the APPLE II case design because it costs $80,000.00 for tooling to make the case. A. 80% of the failures that occur in the field, are caused by plugging the ribbon in improperly. Plugging the ribbon one pin off will cause the LS125 chip to fry and put your disk out of commission.

Q. Can I handle files without a disk? On the cassette tape? A. You need a disk. Q. We have a program that uses illegal line numbers and sets HIMEM. It works fine when loaded from cassette tape but doesn't work loaded from disk. A. I don't know. Q. When you use random access to write on record 97 of a 250 record file, do you mess up records above 97?

A. No, not at all. Q. How do we determine end of file? A. Either put in a special code in the last record and test for it when reading, or reserve the first record of the file for telling your program where the end is. See the ANIMALS program. When you read or write, be sure you start and end with a control D. Q. Any plans to put some kind of joysticks into production? A. No. Q. Are the new HIRES routines done any differently than the old routines? A. While we've had many versions of HIRES they are still being done the same.

Q. Explain the EXEC file. A. It is a sequential text file which contains execute statements. Someone wrote "well, Randy" on the front of the Call-APPLE magazine, referring to the statement I made that you can't convert from Integer to APPLESOFT. The conversion shown doesn't convert TAB to HTAB. I got out of that one. On the APPLESOFT CARDS I gave you HPLOT X, Y to X, Y to X, Y (applause) Q. Do you have a fix for the PIA? A. APPLE has a schematic for a PIA on an interface card.

A. We're working on a General Purpose Serial and a General Purpose Parallel cards. APPLE would like to solicit your comments. Write to APPLE, tell us what you want these cards to be able to do. Q. What about lightpens. A. We've hooked one up and had it working. Q. How many peripheral devices can one APPLE II handle? A. 8 APPLE peripheral cards and 48K. Q. Do you have any X-Y Plotter plans? A. We're working with AXIOM trying to develop an inexpensive plotting device. We're looking into a bit pad too. Approximate cost six to eight hundred dollars. Our product line will be expanding. Q. Will you be expanding to an eight inch floppy? A. Not for the APPLE II. However, we may be getting into hard disk for the APPLE II in 1½ to 2 years. Earlier maybe double density, double sided disks with half a megabyte per drive. Q. COLOR Monitor olans? A. We're talking to 3 manufacturers. Haven't chosen yet.

```
Want to round off your calculations
to the nearest hundreth?
```

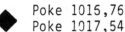

```
Try  N = Int(100*N+.5)/100

This can be put in a DEF FN
statement in Applesoft.
```

```
The easy(?) way to run Basic programs.
```

```
Poke 1015,76
Poke 1017,54
Poke 1018,232
* (hit reset)
* CTRL-Y  (return)
```

WRITE -APPLE

To: Call -Apple

I purchased a set of 16K dynamic ram from "Advanced Computer Products", they passed the memory test in a previous issue of this newsletter. The price was 8 for $200, with a 6 week delay waiting for their "same day shipment", remember to have a set of three 14 pin sockets on hand for your memory select jumpers. Thanks for telling how the Hi Res system handles the colors. I wondered why my blue and green spaceships were dissappearing at certain points on the screen.

Mark Cross
1906 Goodwin Road
Ruston, La. 71270

Dear Mr. Golding:-

Received my July issue of Call -Apple after joining the group. I think you are doing a great job on Call -Apple! In STOPWATCH (Library Pak 1a), the display flickers, this can be fixed by changing Line 190: change POKE 34,22 to POKE 34,24 And I have a question that others might be interested in too: how do you use HIRES with Integer Basic >LOAD without asking the operator to manually enter >HIMEM: 8192? By listing your program, I see a Basic line "5 HIMEM: 16384"; what does this do?

S. H. Lam
256 Hartley Avenue
Pinceton, N. J. 08540

THANKS for your kind comments.
This is not easy to answer in a short space. In fact, if space permits, we will reprint, elsewhere in this issue, an article from Apple's newsletter CONTACT, issue 1, which explains in detail just how to manipulate the program pointers to load a HIRES program in Basic, which is just about what we did in our HIRES demo. What you did not notice was line 0, which disappears, once the program has been run. Again, due to playing games with the program pointer. Line 0 reads: HIMEM: 8192, and if you try to enter it normally, you will get a ***SYNTAX ERR. It was accomplished by first entering the line as "0 PRINT 8192" and then locating the line in memory and changing the PRINT byte ($63) to HIMEM: ($10). Our Programmer's Workshop II is helpful for this, in that it has a routine to locate and display a Basic line as viewed by memory. The HIMEM: 16384 you referred to would have been in the Softcore Software program, which in truth is not a program, but merely a screen display that has been saved on tape. ...ed.

WRITE -APPLE   (Continued)

Dear Call -Apple

I am writing to say I am very impressed with the Call -Apple newsletter. It is not only informative, it is also very useful, particularly the section dealing with the System Monitor and Mini-Assembler, since I am especially interested in Assembly Language. How about making available an Assembly Language Tutorial tape? Also, how would I go about getting a copy of the listing for Integer Basic?

Linda Egan
6471 E. Nixon Street
Lakewood, Ca. 90713

LINDA, if you had made a killing in the stock market, we might be able to get that listing for you. Seriously, that is one very closely guarded secret. And we are looking into the possibility of an Assembly Language Tutorial. ...ed.

DISC DOCUMENTATION FLASH

As we were going to press, we were handed a copy of NEW documentation on Disk II. We are please to report that this documentation, running nearly twice the length of the original. It is far more concise and detailed and has a very good introductory section. So all you gentle folk at Apple Computer we retract (sort of) some of the nasty things we said on page 4 However, we still feel that the Disk II should not have been released until this obviously superior documentation was also ready.
       Val Golding

AND NOW, the ROM...

here is a quickie about setting up the APPLESOFT rom card. First, as the instructions indicated, this card will function only in Slot #0 in your Apple. This card allows you to make a choice of whether you want Integer Basic or Applesoft to be called with control B after you power up. If the switch is in the down position, Integer Basic will be selected. If it is in the up position, Applesoft will be selected. In addition, it is not necessary to change the switch position to call the non-default basic. if the switch is up, hit "reset" and type C080 followed by Control B to get Integer Basic. If the switch is down, hit "reset" and type C080 followed by Control B and return to get Applesoft.

Write -Apple

September's editorial stirred up some interesting responses to Ted Oom's letter concerning the technical level of articles in Call -Apple, some of which are reprinted here. It is our opinion, after reading them, that we should not reduce the level of our article. However, it is also plain that in order to serve our readers best interests, we must also include more articles designed to explain some of the inner workings of the Apple's various routines for beginners, and this we shall do. Read on...

Dear Val:

I have two responses to the letter from Ted Oom which you printed in your editorial. The first is personal: I have also felt the feeling of frustration with technical articles I could not understand. (That includes much of what is in the red Apple II Reference Manual.) However, I have found that after several weeks or months, I have come back to these articles (or the Red Manual), and it suddenly makes sense. Usually it's when I need the information to solve a specific problem. So, my advice to Ted is to save your back issues of Call -Apple. It's a valuable reference.

My second response is a not-too-technical article (especially if you ignore the machine language program) which you might want to print in Call -Apple.

John B. Cook
1905 Bailey Drive
Marshalltown, Iowa 50158

WE APPRECIATE both your letter and the program, which appears elsewhere in this issue

Dear Val and fellow Club Members:

I just got the September issue of Call -Apple. You guys are doing a fantastic job. What a stab in the back for anyone to suggest a lower dues for out of state members. May termites invade their Apples.

I am somewhat up the same tree as Ted <Oom> when it comes to machine language listings and some of the Basic routines found in our newsletter. However, I have every intention of "catching up". I urge you to maintain the course you have set. The only criticism I have is that the magazine doesn't come more often. (I know.) Broaden the scope, yes, but lower it? NO!

THANK YOU RON ALDRICH FOR "CONVERT". I had wondered if such conversion was possible but didn't know where to begin. The program will get a workout when my disk and Applesoft ROM comes in.

Thomas W. DeWinter
Route 2, Box 55
Colona, Il. 61241

WE'RE PRETTY PROUD of Ron and Convert, too!

Mr. Val J. Golding:

I do agree with Ted <Oom> on the direction the club is I do believe you are way, way ahead of me on the technical level. But I've only read the past two issues. In short, I would like to see more simple basic information along with the more technical articles. Perhaps in that way we can all be satisfied. Just don't go too far ahead too soon, remember, as more Apple II's become available to the public, the more beginners you'll have to deal with. After all, Apple II is a personal computer, isn't it?

Library Pak 2 will not auto-run because line 70 (on the Cassette Operating System) reads "CLR: GOTO 0". It should be changed to simply "GOTO 10", since all programs contained on the Library Pak 2 begin with line 10.

Steve Toth
<no address>

AS ALWAYS, your comments are appreciated. earliest copies of Library Pak 2, one line was omitted from each module, which enables the LCOS to function properly. It reads: "0 REM". This is what line 70 on the LCOS menu is actually looking for.

Call -Apple:

With regard to your editorial: I don't agree there is too high a percentage of technical articles in Call -Apple. A smaller number might make it easier to keep track of them for later reference, but I see no other advantage.

Sincerely yours,

Stanley Sawyer
Beau Jardin, Apt. 10-12
2550 Yeager Road
West Lafayette, Ind. 47906

PROF. SAWYER just recently moved from the Seattle area. We're happy to see his continuing interest in the group.

Dear A.P.P.L.E.-

I noticed you have some 8 minute cassettes available to members at six for $5.00. Is this just for Seattle members or can us poor out-of-state-ers buy them also?

I disagree with Ted Oom's suggestion that there might be too many "technical" articles in Call -Apple. You may want to ADD a few more articles which are less oriented toward the computer buff, but don't DROP any of those excellent "technical" articles. I don't understand many of them myself, but I don't think it will be too long before both Ted and I DO start understanding them.

I read in your August issue that I should have "a set of three 14 pin sockets on hand for memory select jumpers" (p5) when I but memory expansion chips. Where can I obtain them?

Gene Bossess
Star Route, Box 220-6
Columbus, Miss. 39701

WE'RE GLAD you asked about the short length cassettes, since we had intended to mention them, and this provides the opportunity. They are manufactured by DAK in Hollywood, and we have used them in audio work for a number of years without any real problems. You can call (800) 423-2636 and get a catalogue and sample tape. To obtain the jumper sockets, contact any of our advertisers.

Call -Apple:

I'd like to comment on the September editorial.

First, Mr Oom is correct, but he is short-sighted. Let us consider why the condition exists. The main reason is the market itself and the new things Apple is selling, i.e., interfaces, Disk II, Rom, etc.

If I had to wait for Apple to provide the excellent service that Goldings & Co. provide, it may be long coming. They provide a service not available ANYwhere else, and I say good job done.

I know it's hard to keep up, but let these things accumulate in your buffer, and lo and behold in a few months you may be glad for their efforts. It is hard in any club to provide for all, but the answer may lie within the club itself. Let the advanced ones help the novice. After all, isn't that what your club is for?

Finally, have you got a sample program to demonstrate how to open a file, write to it, close it and recall same later? If so, would appreciate it.

Ken Hossatt, President
Apple Portland Program Library Exchange
9195 SW Elrose Court
Tigard, Or. 97223

Call -Apple:

Ted Oom is mostly right, but we're all victims of Apple Computer, Inc., not the club. If REAL documentation existed for the computer, instead of that disaster-series "reference manual", the clubs newsletter would be quite appropriate.

Instead, we are forced to either wade through back issues of Byte, DDJ, etc., to find out how to use standard tools. I've never heard of a company including source code in their "reference manual", but no instructions! What do people without the appropriate magazines do?

So it is natural for Ted and some of the rest of us to look to the club for help, not because it's the clubs responsibility, but because we're desperate.

Alan Winston
1771 NW 59th Street - #2
Seattle, Wa. 98107

Dear Mr. Goldings:

Referring to Call -Apple, Vol. I, No. 5, (June), try this subroutine which I use daily:

```
10 IF RD < .005 THEN RD$ = "0.00":RETURN
20 RD = INT(RD*100 + .5)100:rD$ = STR$(RD = .005):
   RD$ = LEFT$(RD$,LEN(RD$)-1):RETURN
```

In main program use:

```
XXX RD = X:GOSUB 10:X$ = RD$
```

This works for positive values of X to 9 digits.

If X can be + or -, then a slower routine is:

```
10 IF ABS(RD) < .005 THEN RD$ = "0.00":RETURN
20 RD = SGN(RD)*INT(ABS(RD)*100+.5)100:
   RD$=STR$(SGN(RD)*ABS(RD)+.005)):
   RD$ =LEFT$(RD$,LEN(RD$)-1):RETURN
```

I hope this may be of some value.

Wilbur C. Andrews
5212 Inglewood La.
Raleigh, NC 27609

WRITE - APPLE

Dear Val,

I noticed that you have a note about the "&". I just got my Applesoft II ROM a month ago and find your notes about undocumented features and tokens helpful.

Another undocumented (in my manual, at least) token is the WAIT. From the listing, it appears to work like this:

WAIT adr, mask, change

will remain in a tight loop reading the location at "adr." When any of the bits at "adr" that are set in mask are not zero, the loop is broken and control goes to the next command. The argument, "change" is optional - any bits set in "change" are changed (from 0 to 1 or 1 to 0) in the word read from "adr" before testing, allowing a test for a change from 1 to 0. In brief, it is

Loop until ((adr). EOR. change) .AND.mask $<>$ 0

It would be normally used to look at an I/O address. For example, WAIT - 16287, 128 delays until the button # 0 is pressed. ('change' is 0 in this example and hence is not needed. WAIT - 16287, 128, 128 loops until button 0 is released!)

Another feature not documented is the DRAW S AT X, Y. The "S" seems to refer to an index of shapes. The routine seems to expect the number of shapes to be in the first two bytes of the table. The next two bytes seem to have an offset from the beginning of the table to the start of the first shape, etc. I haven't tried that yet - perhaps some of your associates have and can confirm or correct.

Richard F. Suitor
166 Tremont Street
Newton, MA 02158

HOW ABOUT IT, Readers? Can you come up with anything?

Dear Mr. Golding:

I'm wondering if you can help me with something.

I'm paralyzed from an accident and wonder if you could ask members if there was any money making ways I could use my Apple computer at home. Can you please find out if anybody could make an automatic phone dialer for the Apple, because I have an idea for a business where I would have to call about 200 persons a day. It would be easier if there was a way of using the computer.

Any help you would give me would be greatly appreciated.

Gerald Schwader
R. 6 Riverside Pk.
Janesville, Wisc. 53545
Phone (608) 756-4006

AGAIN we will ask the readers help.

This is in answer to your editorial in CALL-APPLE of September '78 Vol. 1 No. 8, pg. 7 in which you ask for feedback on the technical level of the articles in CALL-APPLE.

First let me say that the newsletter is terrific! I read and re-read them and try out the programs. I agree that it is good to stretch one's capabilities by learning new techniques.

However, like "Ted" in your editorial, I have been frustrated (even more than mildly) when I read about some new technique or program that looks so useful and interesting and then find that the writer has only hinted at what it was all about and assumes my technical level to be much higher than it actually is. This means I don't understand what the program is supposed to do, why you would want to do it, or how to actually use it. In many cases, a specific example would help. Also a little more hand-holding for us newcomers to the Apple II. In my own case, I have a fair knowledge of 6502 machine language, but on the KIM-I (2 years), not as applied to the Apple.

An example of what I mean is found in Aldrich's tempting hints in Vol. I, No. 6, July '78, pg. 9 on Color Mask Byte. What was this all about? Example?

In general the style and explanations given in System Monitor (July '78, pgs. 12 - 14) is very good. Note that they give examples of how to use the techniques suggested!

Huelsdonk's Free Byte suggestion doesn't work with my 48K Apple II. Some of the calculations are over 32767!

Another case where more information on significance and utility is needed is Dan Chapman's routine on the Video Display, September '78, pg. 4.

Please note that the above comments are meant to be constructive. I really do like the newsletter. But since I am a neophyte, I get frustrated by temptations I can't deal with.

Dr. William R. Dial
438 Roslyn Avenue
Akron, OH 44320

YOUR COMMENTS are appreciated and we will try and follow through.

```
Tired of using the ESC keys for editing?
Hate those gaps when you copy over a
print statement? We have a remedy!
Type Poke 33,33 before listing. Works
in AS and IB.
```

Apple **MONITOR** Program

MONITOR YOUR APPLE II AND LEARN HOW TO

EXAMINE YOUR MEMORY

CHANGE YOUR MEMORY

EDIT

CASSETTE I/O

DEBUGGING AIDS

and

INFORMATION ON THE

MINI-ASSEMBLER

MEMORY TEST

and MORE!

System Monitor

by (and courtesy of) APPLE COMPUTER, INC., Cupertino, Ca.

Introduction

The APPLE II System Monitor is an aid to using your Apple to its fullest capabilities. With this monitor, one may store, examine and execute assembly language programs with a minimum of time and effort.

Previous personal computers required a front panel to enter binary data into memory. This loading process, consisting of setting 8 switches for the data, 16 switches for the address, and another switch for storing, was very time-consuming and extremely monotonous. To set a memory location requires up to 26 toggles on a front panel, in contrast with 8 or fewer keystrokes on the Apple keyboard. This represents a time and effort savings of over one-third.

When your APPLE II is turned on, press the reset key (top row — far right) on the keyboard to use the computer. After you depress the reset key, the speaker will beep, and an "*" (asterisk) prompt character and a flashing cursor will appear on the bottom left of the screen indicating that the computer is ready. The screen will now be in all-text mode with the entire screen of 24 lines of 40 characters each available for display. If this does not happen, the computer is not working properly. The APPLE II system monitor is now ready for use.

Examining Memory

The first use of the monitor is for examining memory. To examine a location in memory, simply type the address followed by a carriage return. The address is one to four hexadecimal digits (0-9 and A-F). For example, type a 0 followed by pressing the carriage return button. The computer will respond by typing the contents of location zero.

Suppose, however, that you wished to examine locations zero to seven. This could be a very time consuming task if you had to type each address on a new line. Instead, you may examine a block of memory by typing the beginning address of the block, followed by a period ("."), followed by the ending address. For example, to examine the memory from location 0 to location 7, type:

0.7 (CR)[1], and

the computer will respond with the data, in order from 0 to 7. Note that when a single location is examined, the computer types the location the data is coming from followed by a dash, followed by the actual data itself and when a range or block of memory is displayed, the computer will display the beginning location, followed by a dash, followed by up to 8 bytes of data, then on the next line it will continue displaying data in this fashion until the end of the range. For example, type:

0.1E (CR)

0000 — 8 bytes of data from 0 to 7
0008 — 8 bytes of data from 8 to F
0010 — 8 bytes of data from 10 to 17
0018 — 7 bytes of data from 18 to 1E

For another example type:

3.7 (CR)

0003 — 5 bytes of data from 3 to 7

Further on we will use the term "address range" to specify a range of memory referred to by "beginning address.ending address". Examples address ranges are:

0.7
3.1E
800.AFFF

In addition, one may use the format ".ending address" to specify an address range beginning at the current address to the specified ending address. For example type:

F000.F006 (CR)

and the computer will respond with:

F000 — A0 00 84 A0 84 4A 84

now type:

.F00E (CR)

and the computer will respond with:

F007 — 4C
F008 — A9 08 85 4B 85 4D E6

Changing Memory

Another important function of the monitor is to alter the contents of memory. To change memory, type the starting address for the data, followed by a colon, followed by the data. Each byte of data must be separated by a space and a carriage return must be entered at the end of the data. For example, type:

        0:00 11 22 33 44 55 66 77 (CR)

Then type:

        0.7 (CR)

to examine the memory locations you just changed. The computer should respond with:

        0000 — 00 11 22 33 44 55 66 77

Note 1.: "(CR)" stands for "depress the carriage return button" and not to type a left parenthesis, the letter C, etc. The carriage return is used to tell Apple that you have finished a line of data.

Note 2.: A control character is typed by holding down the control key (sometimes marked "CTRL") at the same time the specified character is typed. We will use a superscript "C" to indicate a control character thus H^C is a "control H". If you have an Apple supplied keyboard, it will have two additional keys on the second row to the far right. The "←" key performs the same function (backspace) as H^C without depressing the control key; the " →" key is the same as U^C (forward space with copy).

Note 3.: Note that Apple does not display control characters on screen but it will act on them.

Note that the APPLE II keeps track of where the next byte of data is supposed to go, allowing you to type several lines of data at a time. It is recommended that when you enter a program through the monitor, you occasionally check to be sure that you are putting the correct data in the correct locations. To do this, simply enter a small amount of the data, then check the last location deposited into. If the data is misaligned, you must re-enter the last data group. For example, type:

        0:11 2233 44 (CR)

Note that a space was not typed between 22 and 33.

Now type:

        0.3 (CR)

to display contents of 0 to 3.

Location 3 will not be the correct data since it was incorrectly entered and data must be re-entered.

A useful feature of the APPLE II monitor is the "last opened address pointer". When you examine a location, the Apple monitor remembers the location, so that if you type a ":" on the next input line, the data will be entered starting from that location that was just examined. If an address range is examined, the last-opened location is the first address in the range. For example, type:

        0.3 (CR)

The computer will display the contents of locations 0 to 3. Now type:

        :0 11 22 33 (CR)

This deposits data from location 0. Now type again:

        0.3 (CR)

and the computer will respond with:

        0000 — 00 11 22 33

Since the following sections build upon the premise of understanding the above completely, the reader is encouraged to review the above sections if anything presented so far is not clearly understood.

Executing Machine Language Programs

Another important use of the APPLE II monitor is to execute machine language programs as opposed to "BASIC" programs. To execute a program, type the starting address of the program followed by a "G" and a carriage return. The computer will "GO" to the specified location and execute the program there.

You are now ready to run your first assembly-language program through the monitor. This program outputs all of APPLE II's text characters to the screen. Type:

        0:E8 8A 20 ED FD 4C 0 0 (CR)

Now type:

        0.7 (CR)

to check and make sure all data is correct. The computer should type back:

        0000 — E8 8A 20 ED FD 4C 00 00.

Now type:

        0G (CR)

to execute the program. Depress "RESET" button to stop program. The screen now displays APPLE II character set in three modes: normal, inverse and flashing.

Editing Line Entries

When typing an input line on the APPLE II, you are limited to typing 255 characters at a time. Once you have typed 247 characters on a line, the computer will beep each time another character is typed, warning you that you are about to overflow the line. If you do overflow type more than 255 characters, Apple will print a backslash, ignoring everything on that line and you must then re-enter your data.

The Apple II has special editing features that allow you to edit a line as it is being typed in. There are three special functions that allow you to backspace, forward space with pickup, and cancel line. Each is described below:

Backspace

A "control H" (H^C) or the "←" key will move the cursor back one position. (See Note 2). If a character is present in the position it just backed into it will flash that character to indicate the position of the cursor. If another H^C is typed, the cursor will again move back, the character it was on previously will return to normal video (white on black) and the computer will now believe it was never typed. After backspacing the cursor to the character to be changed, type the character it should be.

Forward Space With Copy [2]

A "control U" or the "→" key will copy the current character that the cursor is on from the screen into memory and then advance the cursor one position.

After backspacing to a character and changing it, you may wish to read back in all the characters you just backspaced over. Hold down the "repeat" key as well as U^C or "→" to ease copying. Remember that when a character is backspaced over, it is erased as far as the input line is concerned. When a U^C is typed, the computer reads the character off the screen that the cursor is on. The cursor will then move forward one position. Try it with the example, type:

0:0 15 22 33 44 (no CR)

Now after the second 4, type a control-H or "←" 10 times. The 5 should be flashing. Type a 1, then 9 control-U's or "→". The computer now believes that you typed the line as it now appears.

Note that a control U always uses display for input instead of the keyboard.

Cancel Line

When a control-X is typed during an input, the computer acts as if nothing on the current line had been typed, types a backslash and goes to the next line, waiting for input.

Screen Functions

The backspace and forward space functions move the cursor and modify the input line. With the cursor controls about to be presented, the user may move the cursor anywhere on the screen without modifying the input line. All the cursor move functions consist of typing the escape key, releasing it and then typing the appropriate character. These cursor moves are referred to as "escape-functions" because of the fact that all are preceded by the escape key.

escape A (escape key followed by the A key) moves the cursor forward one space without reading the character as part of the input line.

escape B moves the cursor back one position without erasing any characters from the input line.

escape C moves the cursor down one line without altering the input line the computer sees.

escape D moves the cursor up one line without altering the input line the computer sees.

escape @ returns the cursor to the upper-left-hand corner of the screen and erases the screen.

escape E erases all the characters on the current line from the current cursor position to the end of the line on the screen.

escape F erases all the characters from the current cursor position to the end of the screen.

Error after Carriage Return

In the monitor, if an illegal character is typed, after carriage return is hit, the monitor will do everything up to where the illegal character is typed, then it will beep and stop scanning the line. For example, if you type an illegal Hex number while depositing data into memory, the monitor will store all data typed before the illegal digit, then it will stop depositing data and beep the speaker

Multiple Operations

An exclusive feature of the APPLE II monitor is the ability to do several things on one input line before pressing carriage return, except during a store operation. For example, to examine the blocks of memory from 0 to 7 and from 300 to 31F, type:

0.7 300.31F (CR)

Note that the two address ranges are separated by a blank. To perform multiple commands per line, each command must be separated from the previous command by at least one blank. Single character commands need not be separated by a space; thus LLL (CR) is legal.

When the Apple monitor is expecting an address, it will examine only the last four digits typed for the address if more than four digits were typed. For example, 2300 is the same as 12300, since in the second case the Apple will only "see" the 2300. Similarly, when the monitor is expecting a data byte, it will only examine the last two digits if more than two digits were typed. This is a useful way to correct errors quickly without backspacing.

Cassette Input/Output

To read an address range of data or a machine language program from a cassette tape, type the address range followed by an R, start the tape recorder playing, and press carriage return. Example:

300.3FFR (start cassette in play mode) (press carriage return)

will read the address range from 300 to 3FF inclusive from the tape.

If there is a bad tape read, (determined by a checksum byte at the end of each record) the monitor will type the letters "ERR". At the completion of reading a record or address range off of the tape, the speaker will beep and a "*" and a flashing cursor will appear indicating that the read is finished.

To write an address range onto the cassette, type the address range followed by the letter W. Press record on the cassette recorder, then press return. The speaker will beep upon completion of the write. Example 2:

> 300.3FFW (start cassette in record mode) (press carriage return)

will write the address range from 300 to 3FF on to the tape.

Example 3:

> 300.3FFW 800.8A0W (start cassette in record mode) (press carriage return)

will write the range from 300 to 3FF, then will write the range from 800 to 8A0 onto tape.

Definition of a record on the cassette is an address range written on the cassette, preceded by a 6 second header. A record may be of any length from 1 byte to 48K-bytes (maximum size of the system).

Memory Move ("M")

Occasionally it becomes necessary to move a block of memory to another address range. For example, after writing a record onto cassette, you may desire to check if the write was good by reading the data back out. You would simply write the tape, copy the current memory range to another block of memory, and try reading your program back in. If the read is good, everything is fine. If not, move the correct data back into the original range, and start over.

To move memory, type the beginning destination address followed by a less-than sign, "<", followed by the address range to move and the letter "M" for "MOVE". For example:

> 800 <300.3FFM (CR)

will copy location 300 to location 800, location 301 to location 801, etc. through 3FF to 8FF.

The above line should be read as eight hundred from three hundred to three F F move.

Another use of the memory move is to set a range of memory to a specific value, such as zero. To do this, set the first location of the range to the value, then type the second location of the range, followed by a "<", the first location of the range, a ".", and the next to last address in the range. For example, to zero locations 800 to 8FF type:

> 800:0 (CR)
> 801 <800.8FEM (CR)

What the above does is copy location 800 to 801, 801 to 802, 802 to 803, etc. up to 8FD to 8FE, then 8FE to 8FF.

Memory Verify ("V")

Sometimes it is useful to check two ranges of memory to see if they are identical. The format for doing this is similar to moving memory, but instead of a M, a V should be typed. For example, to check if the range from 300 to 3FF contains the same data as 800 to 8FF, type:

> 300 <800.8FFV (CR)

This will compare location 300 to 800, then 301 to 801, etc. If two corresponding locations match, the verify continues on to the next two corresponding locations; if on the otherhand, location 305 contained an F7 while location 805 contained an FF, the following would be printed:

> 305 — F7 (FF)

indicating that a non-match was discovered.

Miscellaneous Commands

The APPLE II display system has three modes of displaying characters: normal video (white on black), inverse video (black on white), and flashing (alternates between normal and inverse). Through the monitor, you can specify either normal or inverse mode for monitor output. Monitor input is always printed in normal video. By typing an N on an input line, the monitor will output in normal video. By typing an I on an input line, the monitor will output in inverse video. For example, type:

> 0.1F I .3F N (CR)

The monitor will display locations 0 to 1F, switch to inverse video mode, display locations 20 to 3F, then switch back to normal video mode.

The APPLE II computer comes supplied with BASIC in ROM. To enter BASIC type a control-B in the monitor and a carriage return, and you will be in BASIC. To return to the monitor, hit the reset key. If you hit the reset key while in BASIC and wish to re-enter BASIC without destroying your program, type a control-C and depress return key and you will be back in BASIC.

By typing a control-Y on a line, the APPLE II monitor does a jump to location 3F8. This is supplied mainly to save typing time. For example, by putting a jump instruction at location 3F8, you can do a "GO" to any location in memory with one keystroke. Y^C may also be used for user programs requiring up to three arguments.

To specify a port for keyboard input, type a single digit (0-7) followed by a control-K to specify I/O slot number. The default port is port number 0, or the keyboard not slot 0.

To specify a port for output, type a single digit (0-7) representing the I/O port number, followed by a control-P. Default output port is 0, or the screen and not slot 0.

Debugging Aids

The process between writing a program and making it actually work is called debugging. Assembly language programs over 20 bytes long will most probably require debugging. The following monitor section describes several features of the monitor for quick and easy debugging.

After entering a program, you may desire to examine a certain portion of the program in 6502 mnemonics instead of the machine code. To list out memory in Mnemonic, type the starting address of the part you wish to list out, followed by the letter "L" and a carriage return. The monitor will list the next 20 mnemonic instructions starting at the address specified.

Four output fields are generated for each disassembled instruction: (1) Address of first byte of instruction in Hex; (2) Hex object code listing of instruction, from 1 to 3 bytes long; (3) 3-character mnemonic, or ??? for undefined opcodes· (which assume a length of one byte); (4) address field, in one of the following formats:

Format	Address Mode
-empty-	Invalid, Implied, or Accumulator
$12	Page zero
$1234	Absolute or branch target
#$12	Immediate
$12,X	Zero page, indexed by X
$12,Y	Zero page, indexed by Y
$1234,X	Absolute, indexed by X
$1234,Y	Absolute, indexed by Y
($1234)	Absolute indirect
($12),X	Indexed indirect
($12),Y	Indirect indexed

Note that unlike MOS Technology assemblers, which use "A" for accumulator addressing, the Apple disassembler outputs an empty field to avoid confusion and facilitate byte counting. Upon displaying twenty instructions, if another "L" and carriage return are typed, the next twenty instructions will be disassembled.

For an example of the "L" (list) command type:

    F000L (CR)

and Apple will respond with:

F000-	A0	00	LDY	#$00
F002-	84	A0	STY	$A0
F004-	84	4A	STY	$4A
F006-	84	4C	STY	$4C
F008-	A9	08	LDA	#$08
F00A-	85	4B	STA	$4B
F00C-	85	4D	STA	$4D
F00E-	E6	4D	INC	$4D
F010-	B1	4C	LDA	($4C),Y
F012-	49	FF	EOR	#$FF
F004-	91	4C	STA	($4C),Y
F016-	D1	4C	CMP	($4C),Y
F018-	D0	0X	BNE	$F022
F01A-	49	FF	EOR	#$FF
F01C-	91	4C	STA	($4C),Y
F01E-	D1	4C	CMP	($4C),Y
F020-	F0	EC	BEQ	$F00E
F022-	4C AD E5		JMP	$E5AD
F025-	4C 79 F1		JMP	$F179
F028-	20 32 F0		JSR	$F032

*

Single Stepping

Another useful debugging aid is single-stepping. Single-stepping allows the user to execute the program, one step at a time, while watching the registers as the program is executed. To single step, type the address to begin single-stepping, followed by an "S" and carriage return. The monitor will execute the instruction at that location, then display the instruction in disassembled format, (see above), followed by a display of the registers in the format:

    A=BB X=BB Y=BB P=BB S=BB

where BB represents a Hexadecimal byte. P stands for processor status, and S stands for stack pointer. To use the processor status byte, see processor status register section of the MOS Technology Software Manual. To execute the next program instruction, simply type another "S" and (return).

During single-stepping, you may desire to change the contents of the registers. To do so, after the registers are displayed, type a ":" (colon) followed by the data to go into the A register, followed by data for the X Register (if desired), followed in order the registers were displayed. To display the contents of the registers, type a control-E followed by a carriage return[2] For example, suppose the registers were displayed as:

    A=01 X=2E Y=53 P=78 S=AC

to change A to 00 and X to 30, type:

    :0 30

Then, if you typed a control-E to examine the registers, the following would be displayed:

    A=00 X=30 Y=53 P=78 S=AC

For an example of single step ("S") command, retype in our previous program example:

    0: E8 8A 20 ED FD 4C 0 0 (CR)

Now type:

    0S (CR)

and the computer will respond:

```
0000-    E8              INX
 A=06  X=07  Y=0B  P=30  S=6D
```

The 6502 registers are now open; change the A and X registers by typing:

```
    :A FF (CR)
```

Now type a·control-E and a carriage return to re-examine the registers. Apple will respond with:

```
*
  A=0A  X=FF  Y=0B  P=30  S=6D
```

Type "S" and carriage return a few more times to explore "single-stepping".

```
*S
0001-    8A              TXA
 A=FF  X=FF  Y=0B  P=B0  S=6D
*S
0002-    20 ED FD        JSR $FDED
 A=FF  X=FF  Y=0B  P=B0  S=6D
*S
FDED-    6C 36 00        JMP ($0036)
 A=FF  X=FF  Y=0B  P=B0  S=6D
```

Multiple Stepping

Another tool for debugging is the BRK instruction. In the APPLE II, any time a BRK instruction is encountered, it acts as if the BRK instruction were just single-stepped, and goes into the monitor, where you may continue single-stepping or whatever you want to do. Note that although BRK is only one byte ($00), the 6502 microprocessor treats it as a two-byte instruction. Therefore, to properly use the BRK instruction, you should put the BRK instruction at the point you wish to start single-stepping from, execute your program, and when the program encounters the BRK instruction, it will return to the monitor as described above. Then you should replace the BRK instruction with the original instruction, and initialize single-stepping from that point.

Tracing

Another debugging tool is the trace ("T") command. This command executes a program, instruction by instruction, and as it executes each instruction, it displays the instruction in single-step format. Trace will continue tracing until either a BRK instruction is encountered or the reset key is hit. Example:

```
0T (CR)
```

will "trace" a program starting at location 0.

```
0000-    E8              INX
 A=07  X=07  Y=00  P=30  S=12
0001-    8A              TXA
 A=07  Y=07  Y=00  P=30  S=12
0002-    20 ED FD        JSR $FDED
 A=07  Y=07  Y=00  P=30  S=12
FDED-    6C 36 00        JMP = ($0036
 A=07  Y=07  Y=00  P=30  S=12
03B9-    84 35           STY $35
 A=07  Y=07  Y=00  P=30  S=10
038B-    48              PHA
 A=07  Y=07  Y=00  P=30  S=0F
038C-    20 A5 03        JSR $03A5
 A=07  Y=07  Y=00  P=30  S=0F
03A5-    A0 0B           LDY = #$0B
 A=07  Y=07  Y=00  P=30  S=0D
03A7-    18              CLC
 A=07  Y=07  Y=00  P=30  S=0D
03A8-    48              PHA
 A=
*
```

The above trace would have continued until a "BR command was encountered, but we stopped it hitting the "RESET" key.

The above described the usage of the monit directly from the keyboard. In addition to the abov the monitor contains many useful subroutines th can be utilized in your programs.

WHAT... LIBRARY PAKS AGAIN ?

Yes, again! We have been asked by members who hav chased Library Pak 1A, whether they should order Pak 1B. answer to this one is no. The letter designates only modifications have been made. In this case, one progra removed and another updated. Should you want an updated c any program or Pak, we will do that for just a $2.00 ha charge. Assuming we let you in on it!!!

INTEGER BASIC FLOATING POI

We admit at last to having Don Williams' Integer routines actually in our hands, and guarantee herewith they will be published in the September Call -Apple. We have complete program listings and supporting documentati

...And speaking of what's coming up in Call -Apple certainly like to be able to print your software and cles. How about it, out there?

Apple II Mini-Assembler

The following section covers use of the Apple II mini-assembler only. It is not a course in assembly language programming. The following section assumes the user has a working knowledge of 6502 programming and mnemonics. The Apple II mini-assembler is a programming aid aimed at reducing the amount of time required to convert a handwritten program to object code. The mini-assembler is basically a look-up table for opcodes. With it, you can type mnemonics with their absolute addresses, and the assembler will convert it to the correct object code and store it in memory.

Typing "F666G" will put the user in mini-assembler mode. While in this mode, any line typed in will be interpreted as an assembly language instruction, assembled, and stored in binary form unless the first character on the command line is a "$".

If it is, the remainder of the line will be interpreted as a normal monitor command, executed, and control returned to assembler mode. To get out of the assembler mode, reset must be pushed.

If the first character on the line is blank, the assembled instruction will be stored starting at the address immediately following the previously assembled instruction. If the first character is nonblank (and not "$"), the line is assumed to contain an assembly language instruction preceded by the instruction address (a hex number followed by a ":"). In either case, the instruction will be retyped over the line just entered in disassembler format to provide a visual check of what has been assembled. The counter that keeps track of where the next instruction will be stored is the pseudo PC (Program Counter) and it can be changed by many monitor commands (eg., 'L', 'T',...). Therefore, it is advisable to use the explicit instruction address mode after every monitor command and, of course, when the mini-assembler is first entered.

Errors (unrecognized mnemonic, illegal format, etc.) are signalled by a "beep" and a carrot ("^") will be printed beneath the last character read from the input line by the mini-assembler.

The mnemonics and formats accepted by the mini-assembler are the same as those listed by the 6502 Programmers Manual, with the following exceptions and differences:

1. All imbedded blanks are ignored, except inside addresses.

2. All addresses typed in are assumed to be in hex (rather than decimal or symbolic). A preceding "$" (indicating hex rather than decimal or symbolic) is therefore optional, except that it should not precede the instruction address.

3. Instructions that operate on the accumulator have a blank operand field instead of "A".

4. When entering a branch instruction, following the branch mnemonic should be the target of the branch. If the destination address is not known at the time the instruction is entered, simply enter an address that is in the neighborhood, and later re-enter the branch instruction with the correct target address. NOTE: If a branch target is specified that is out of range, the mini-assembler will flag the address as being in error.

5. The operand field of an instruction can only be followed by a comment field, which starts with a semi-colon (";"). Obviously, the mini-assembler ignores the field and in fact will type over it when the line is typed over in disassembler format. This "feature" is included only to be compatible with future upgrades including input sources other than the keyboard.

6. Any page zero references will generate page zero instruction formats if such a mode exists. There is no way to force a page zero address to be two bytes, even if the address has leading zeros.

In general, to specify an addressing type, simply enter it as it would be listed in the disassembly. For information on the disassembler, see Apple II System Monitor in the previous section. A complete listing of the mini-assembler appears at the end of this section. An example of the mini-assembler appears below. Note that the second "BRK" has no space before it hence Apple refused the input, sounded the bell and typed a "↑" underneath the "R". In "LDA3R45", Apple also refused the instruction because "R" is not a legal hex digit. Remember to hit the "RESET" key to get out of the mini-assembler.

```
*F666G

!0: INX

0000-      E8              INX
! TXA

0001-      8A              TXA
! JSR  $FDED

0002-      20 ED FD        JSR     $FDED
! JMP  $0

0005-      4C 00 00        JMP     $0000
! BRK

0008-      00              BRK
!BRK
  ↑
! BRK

0009-      00              BRK
! LDA  3R45
        ↑
!
```

```
0010  :           THIS PROGRAM TESTS MEMORY BY LOADING EACH LOCATION
0020  :        WITH 55, TESTING, LOADING WITH AA, AND TESTING.
0030  :        IF ANY LOCATION IS BAD, THE PROGRAM RINGS THE BELL
0040  :        AND STOPS.  THE OFFENDING ADDRESS WILL BE SHOWN
0050  :        IN LOCATIONS 02 AND 03.
0060  :           START BY LOADING LOCATIONS AS FOLLOWS
0070  :     02 - LO BYTE OF START ADDRESS
0080  :     03 - HI BYTE OF START ADDRESS
0090  :     04 - LO BYTE OF END ADDRESS
0100  :     05 - HI BYTE OF END ADDRESS
0110  :     TYPICAL ENTRY *02:00 08 FF 3F  FOR 16K MACHINE
0120  STLO  .DL 0002
0130  STHI  .DL 0003
0140  ENLO  .DL 0004
0150  ENHI  .DL 0005
0160  BELL  .DL FF3A      BELL IN MONITOR
0170        .OR 0300      START ADDR

0180  TEST LDY 00         ZERO Y        ;0300   A000
0190  LOAD LDA 55         BI 01010101   ;0302   A955
0200       STA (STLO),Y   55 TO MEM     ;0304   9102
0210       CMP (STLO),Y   IS IT THERE?  ;0306   D102
0220       BNE ERR        ERR IF NOT    ;0308   D01D
0230       LDA 0AA        TO 10101010   ;030A   A9AA
0240       STA (STLO),Y   TO MEM        ;030C   9102
0250       CMP (STLO),Y   IS IT THERE?  ;030E   D102
0260       BNE ERR        ERR IF NOT    ;0310   D015
0270       JSR INCR       TO INCR ROUT  ;0312   201803
0280       BCC LOAD       BACK TO LOAD  ;0315   90EB
0290       RTS            TO APPLE MON  ;0317   60
0300  INCR LDA *STLO      THIS ROUTINE  ;0318   A502
0310       CMP *ENLO      INCREMENTS    ;031A   C504
0320       LDA *STHI      THE MEMORY    ;031C   A503
0330       SBC *ENHI      LOCATION      ;031E   E505
0340       INC *STLO                    ;0320   E602
0350       BNE RTN                      ;0322   D002
0360       INC *STHI                    ;0324   E603
0370  RTN  RTS            GO DO AGAIN   ;0326   60
0380  ERR  JSR BELL                     ;0327   203AFF
0390       BRK            HALT-SEE 02,03;032A   00
0400  :     ENDING ADDRESSES FOR LOCATIONS 04 AND 05
0410  : 4K-0FFF 16K-3FFF 32K-7FFF 48K-BFFF
0420  :     TO RUN,    *300G
0430  : YOU MAY SEE THE AA LOADED MEMORY BY - *800.3FFF 'RETURN'
0440  : FOR 16K. THIS PROGRAM DOES NOT TEST THE 1ST 2K.
0450        .EN
```

```
SYMBOL TABLE
STLO    0002
STHI    0003
ENLO    0004
ENHI    0005
BELL    FF3A
TEST    0300
LOAD    0302
INCR    0318
RTN     0326
ERR     0327
```

AN APPLE II MEMORY TEST
by Bob Huelsdonk

I wrote this simple program to test new memory chips I bought. Just store the correct end address for your Apple in locat'ns 4 & 5, run 300G and display 800 to the end.

25

Apple II Software

CS-4002. Sports Games-1. Four exciting graphics games. Includes an amazing **Baseball** game for two players who control infielders and outfielders, type of pitch, and the swing of the bat. Even has sacrifices, double plays, and home runs. **Horse Race** allows up to eleven players to bet on the outcome of a horse race. **Slalom** challenges you to ski through the gates in a minimum time. In **Darts** you try to throw your darts as close to the bullseye as possible by controlling the game paddles. $7.95.

CS-4003. Strategy Games-1. Play **Checkers*** in color against the Apple. **Skunk** is a dice game for one or two players. **UFO** is a space game in which you must outwit an enemy spaceship. **Blockade** with exciting graphics and sound effects, with a one or two player option. **Genius,** a challenging trivia quiz. *Requires Applesoft BASIC. $7.95.

CS-4201. CAI Programs-1. US Map asks you to identify states and their capitals. **Spelling** helps the user study a list of words he has previously entered. **Math Drill** for simple arithmetic problems. **Add-With-Carry** is a sophisticated tool for teaching addition of two and three place numbers by helping the student work the problem digit by digit, adjust to the student's level of skill. $7.95.

CS-4001. Space Games-1. Four color-graphics programs for your Apple, including **Rocket Pilot** an advanced lunar lander simulation in which you guide your spacecraft over the mountain to a safe landing on the opposite side. In **Saucer Invasion,** you protect the earth by shooting down the alien invasion fleet with your missile launcher. In **Star Wars,** you line up the Tie fighters in your sights and fire before they get away. **Dynamic Bouncer** is a color graphics demonstration program for your Apple which fills the screen with colored walls that appear and disappear at random, while a ball bounces around within. $7.95.

creative computing software

CS-4301. Know Yourself (4 Programs). Life Expectancy — will a different life style increase your life expectancy? **Psychotherapy** — analyze symptoms in your feelings and behavior to determine your mental health. **Computer Literacy** — what's yours? **Alcohol** — effect of alcohol on your behavior. $7.95.

Blank Cassettes

CT-C8. Blank C-8 cassettes with 4 minutes of tape per side. Perfect for one or two programs. Highest quality tape packaged in nifty red translucent cassettes in soft plastic box. $1.00 ea., 5 for $4.00.

To Order...

Creative Computing Software should be stocked by your local retail computer store. If your favorite outlet doesn't yet offer it, have him call C.J. at 800-631-8112. (In NJ, 201-540-0445).

Or you can order directly from Creative Computing. Send your check for tapes plus $1.00 shipping and handling per order to Creative Computing Software, P.O. Box 789-M, Morristown, NJ 07960. NJ residents add 5% sales tax. Visa or Master Charge are acceptable also. For faster service, call in your bank card order toll free to 800-631-8112. (In NJ, 201-540-0445).

Apple II Reseller Store Listing

ALABAMA
COMPUTERLAND
HUNTSVILLE, AL
(205) 539-1200

LOGIC STORE
OPELIKA, AL
(205) 745-7735

ARIZONA
BYTE SHOP
PHOENIX, AZ
(602) 265-0065

BYTE SHOP
TEMPE, AZ
(602) 894-1129

BYTE SHOP
TUSCON, AZ
(602) 327-4579

CALIFORNIA
BYTE SHOP
CITRUS HEIGHTS, CA
(916) 961-2983

BYTE SHOP
LAWNDALE, CA
(408) 371-2421

BYTE SHOP
SAN JOSE, CA
(408) 377-4685

CAPITAL COMPUTER
DAVIS, CA
(916) 758-1780

COMPUTER CENTER
SAN DIEGO, CA
(714) 292-5302

COMPUTER DEMO RM
SAN RAFAEL, CA
(415) 457-9311

COMPUTER MERCHANT
SAN DIEGO, CA
(714) 293-7730

COMPUTER STORE
SANTA MONICA, CA
(213) 451-0036

COMPUTERLAND
SAN LEANDRO, CA
(415) 895-9363

COMPUTERLAND
DUBLIN, CA
(415) 828-8090

COMPUTERLAND
EL CERRITO, CA
(415) 233-5010

COMPUTERLAND
HAYWARD, CA
(415) 538-8080

COMPUTERLAND
LOS ALTOS, CA
(415) 941-8154

COMPUTERLAND
MISSON VIEJO, CA
(714) 560-9912

COMPUTERLAND
SAN BERNADINO, CA
(714) 886-6838

COMPUTERLAND
SAN DIEGO, CA
(714) 560-9912

COMPUTERLAND
SAN FRANCISCO, CA
(415) 546-1592

COMPUTERLAND
SAN MATEO, CA
(415) 572-8080

COMPUTERLAND
LAWNDALE, CA
(213) 371-7144

COMPUTERLAND
THOUSAND OAKS, CA
(805) 495-3554

COMPUTERLAND
TUSTIN, CA
(714) 544-0542

COMPUTERLAND
WALNUT CREEK, CA
(415) 935-6502

COMPUTERLAND
INGLEWOOD, CA
(213) 766-8080

JADE COMPUTER
HAWTHORNE, CA
(213) 679-3313

COLORADO
COMPUTER TECH.
DENVER, CO
(303) 427-4438

COMPUTERLAND
DENVER, CO
(303) 759-4685

CONNECTICUT
COMPUTERLAND
FAIRFIELD, CT
(203) 374-2227

DELAWARE
COMPUTERLAND
NEWARK, DE
(302) 738-9656

DISTRICT OF COL.
GEORGETOWN COMPUTER
WASHINGTON, DC
(202) 337-6545

FLORIDA
MICRO COMPUTER
SO. DAYTONA, FL
(904) 767-1319

COMPUTER AGE
POMPANO BEACH, FL
(305) 946-4999

GEORGIA
COMPUTERLAND
SMYRNA, GA
(404) 953-0406

THE LOGIC STORE
COLUMBUS, GA
(404) 568-0197

ROY ABELL & ASSOC.
COLUMBUS, GA
(404) 568-0080

ILLINOIS
COMPUTERLAND
ARLINGTON HTS., IL
(312) 255-6488

COMPUTERLAND
NILES, IL
(312) 967-1714

ILLINI MICRO
NAPERVILLE, IL
(312) 420-8813

COMPUTERLAND
OAK LAWN, IL
(312) 422-8080

INDIANA
DATA DOMAIN
BLOOMINGTON, IN
(812) 334-3607

IOWA
MEMORY BANK
DAVENPORT, IA
(319) 386-3330

KANSAS
COMPUTER SYSTEM
WICHITA, KS
(316) 265-1120

COMPUTERLAND
OVERLAND PARK, KS
(913) 492-8882

KENTUCKY
COMPUTERI AND
LOUISVILLE, KY
(502) 425-8303

PRAGMA TECH.
LOUISVILLE, KY
(502) 895-1230

LOUISIANA
MICRO COMPUTER
NEW ORLEANS, LA
(504) 821-0870

MARYLAND
COMPUTERS UNLIMITED
TOWSON, MD
(301) 321-1553

COMPUTERLAND
ROCKVILLE, MD
(301) 948-7676

MASSACHUSETTS
COMPUTER MART
WALTHAM, MA
(617) 899-4540

CPU SHOP
CHARLESTOWN, MA
(617) 242-3350

MICHIGAN
COMPUTER MART
ROYAL OAK, MI
(313) 576-0900

COMPUTERLAND
KENTWOOD, MI
(616) 942-2931

COMPUTERLAND
SOUTHFIELD, MI
(313) 356-8111

HOBBY ELEC.
FLINT, MI
(313) 743-2220

NEWMAN COMPUTER
ANN ARBOR, MI
(313) 994-3200

TRI-CITIES COMPUTER MART
SAGINAW, MI
(517) 790-1360

UNITED MICRO SYSTEMS
ANN ARBOR, MI
(313) 668-6806

MINNESOTA
COMPUTERLAND
BLOOMINGTON, MN
(612) 884-1474

MISSOURI
COMPUTERLAND
SPRINGFIELD, MO
(417) 883-7085

NEBRASKA
OMAHA COMPUTER
OMAHA, NB
(402) 592-3590

NEW HAMPSHIRE
COMPUTERLAND
NASHUA, NH
(603) 889-5238

COMPUTER MART
NASHUA, NH
(603) 883-2386

NEW JERSEY
COMPUTER LABS
BUDDLAKE, NJ
(201) 691-1984

COMPUTER MART
ISELIN, NJ
(201) 283-0600

COMPUTERLAND
MORRISTOWN, NJ
(201) 539-4077

NEW YORK
COMPUTERLAND
BUFFALO, NY
(716) 836-6511

COMPUTERLAND
ITHACA, NY
(607) 277-4888

COMPUTER MART
NEW YORK, NY
(212) 686-7923

COMPU WORLD INC.
ROCHESTER, NY
(716) 473-5790

MINI-MICRO MART
SYRACUSE, NY
(315) 422-4467

OHIO
COMPUTERLAND
MAYFIELD HTS., OH
(216) 461-1200

CYBERSHOP MICRO
COLUMBUS, OH
(614) 239-8081

DAYTON COMPUTER
DAYTON, OH
(513) 296-1248

21ST CENTURY SHOP
CINCINNATI, OH
(513) 651-2111

OKLAHOMA
VERN ST. PRODUCTS
PAPULPA, OK
(918) 224-4260

OREGON
COMPUTER PATHWAYS
SALEM, OR
(503) 363-8929

COMPUTERLAND PORTLD.
TIGARD, OR
(503) 620-6170

REAL OREGON COMPUTER
EUGENE, OR
(503) 484-1040

PENNSYLVANIA
COMPUTER AID
LATROBE, PA
(412) 539-1133

COMPUTERLAND
MECHANICSBURG, PA
(717) 763-1116

MICROTRONICS
PHILADELPHIA, PA
(800) 523-4550

TEXAS
BYTE SHOP
RICHARDSON, TX
(214) 234-5955

COMPUTERLAND
AUSTIN, TX
(512) 452-5701)

COMPUTERLAND
HOUSTON, TX
(713) 977-0909

INTERACTIVE COMPUTER
HOUSTON, TX
(713) 772-5257

MICRO MIKE'S
AMARILLO, TX
(806) 372-3633

MICRO MART
SAN ANTONIO, TX
(512) 222-1427

UTAH
HOME COMPUTER CENTER
SALT LAKE CITY, UT
(801) 484-6502

VIRGINIA
COMPUTER PLACE
ROANOKE, VA
(703) 982-3661

COMPUTER SYSTEMS
MCLEAN, VA
(703) 821-8333

COMPUTER PLUS
ALEXANDRIA, VA
(703) 751-5656

WASHINGTON
COMPUTERLAND
BELLEVUE, WA
(206) 746-2070

COMPUTERLAND
FEDERAL WAY, WA
(206) 838-9363

COMPUTERLAND
TACOMA, WA
(206) 581-0388

EMPIRE ELECTRONICS
SEATTLE, WA
(206) 244-5200

WEST VIRGINIA
MICRO DATA SYSTEMS
OSAGE, WV
(304) 599-5121

WISCONSIN
BYTE SHOP
GREENFIELD, WI
(414) 281-7004

COMPUTERLAND
MADISON, WI
(608) 273-2020

COMPUTERLAND
MILWAUKEE, WI
(414) 466-8990

HAWAII
MICROCOMPUTER
HONOLULU, HI
(808) 536-5288

CANADA
OMEGA COMPUTING
TORONTO, ONT.
(416) 425-9200

BMB CANADA
MILTON, ONT.
(416) 878-7890

Basically Speaking

INTEGER BASIC

APPLESOFT BASIC

TOKENS CHART

MEMORY MAPS

CONVERTING IB TO AS

CONVERTING OLD AS TO AS II

LINKAGE ROUTINES

AS TONE ROUTINE

SAVE MEMORY ON A STRING

PEEKS, POKES, AND CALLS

RESURECTING THE DEAD (AS PROGRAMS)

AS FORMATTING

HEX CONVERTING

HANDY LIST OF CALLS

and MORE!

APPLE II BASIC STRUCTURE

by Steve Wozniak

Apple Computer, Inc.

(Reprinted from Dr. Dobbs Journal of Computer Calisthenics and Orhtodontia, Box E, Menlo Park, Ca. 94025, Issue No. 23)

An understanding of the internal representation of a BASIC program is necessary in order to develop ... algorithms. Fig. 1 illustrates the significant pointers for a program in memory. Variable and symbol table assignment begins at the location whose address is contained in the pointer LOMEM ($4A and $4B where '$' stands for hex). This is $800 (2048) on the APPLE-II unless changed by the user with the LOMEM: command. A second pointer, PV (Variable Pointer, at $CC and $CD) contains the address of the location immediately following the last location allocated to variables. PV is equal to LOMEM if no variables are actively assigned as is the case after a NEW, CLR, or LOMEM: command. As variables are assigned, PV increases.

Figure 1 - MEMORY MAP

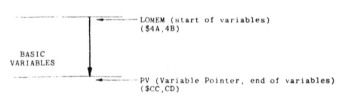
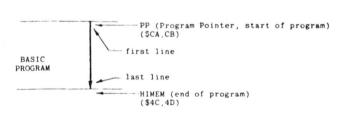

The BASIC program is stored beginning with the lowest numbered line at the location whose address is contained in the pointer PP (Program Pointer, at $CA and $CB). The pointer HIMEM ($4C and $4D) contains the address of the location immediately following the last byte of the last line of the program. This is normally the top of memory unless changed by the user with the HIMEM: command. As the program grows, PP decreases. PP is equal to HIMEM if there is no program in memory. Adequate checks in the BASIC insure that PV never exceeds PP. This is essence says that variables and program are not permitted to overlap.

Lines of a BASIC program are not stored as they were originally entered (in ASCII) on the APPLE-II due to a pre-translation stage. Internally each line begins with a length byte which may serve as a link to the next line. The length byte is immediately followed by a two-byte line number stored in binary, low-order byte first. Line numbers range from 0 to 32767. The line number is followed by 'items' of various types, the final of which is an 'end-of-line' token ($01). Refer to Figure 2.

Figure 2 - LINE REPRESENTATION

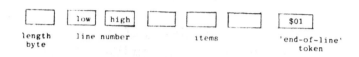

Single bytes of value less than $80 (128) are 'tokens' generated by the translator. Each token stands for a fixed unit of text as required by the syntax of the language BASIC. Some stand for keywords such as PRINT or THEN while others stand for punctuation or operators such as ',' or '+'.

Integer constants are stored as three consecutive bytes. The first contains $B0-$B9 (ASCII '0'-'9') signifying that the next two contain a binary constant stored low-order byte first. The line number itself is not preceeded by $B0-$B9. All constants are in this form including line number references such as 500 in the statement GOTO 500. Constants are always followed by a token. Although one or both bytes of a constant may be positive (less than $80) they are not tokens.

Variable names are stored as consecutive ASCII characters with the high order bit set. The first character is between $C1 and $DA (ASCII 'A' – 'Z'), distinguishing names from constants. All names are terminated by a token which is recognizable by a clear high-order bit. The '$' in string names such as A$ is treated as a token.

String constants are stored as a token of value $28 followed by ASCII text (with high-order bits set) followed by a token of value $29. REM statements begin with the REM token ($5D) followed by ASCII text (with high-order bits set) followed by the 'end-of-line' token.

Figure 3 - ITEMS

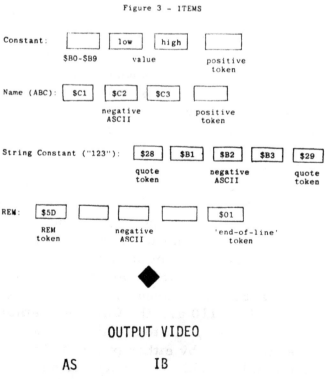

◆

OUTPUT VIDEO

	AS	IB
Normal		Poke 50,255
Flash		Poke 50,127
Inverse		Poke 50,63

APPLESOFT II POINTERS & TOKENS
by Val Golding

Applesoft & Applesoft II store in memory from the bottom up, unlike Integer Basic, which is just the opposite, storing from the top down. Although pointers and characteristics of Applesoft I and II are similar, they are different. Therefore we will limit ourselves to APII in this discussion.

Programs store starting at decimal location 12289 upwards, and variables are located starting at the high end of program storage. When there is no program present, then the variables will start at 12291. String variables, however, store downwards from the top of memory, 16384 for a 16K Apple.

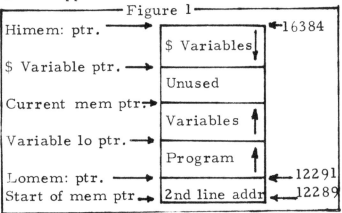

Figure 1

Applesoft has a somewhat complex group of pointers; we're not positive we have covered them all here. All pointers are given in decimal form. 103 & 104 are the start of memory pointer. They always point to 12289 where you can find the address of the second program statement. They are not affected by setting LOMEM:. 105 & 106 are the variable low pointer. They point to the next available location available for either more program or variables. 107 & 108 are the variable pointer. They point to the last location used by variables, plus one. 109 & 110 are the Current Memory pointer. They point to the highest location plus one, used by either program or variables. 111 & 112 are the low string pointer. They point to the next location available for string variable storage. 115 & 116 are the HIMEM: pointer. They always point to HIMEM: which is the first location

available for string variable storage. Finally, we have the true program pointer, 175 & 176. These point to the highest location, plus one, used by the program. They are NOT affected by the setting of LOMEM:.

A program to display Applesoft II tokens is listed in column 2. Unlike Integer Basic, which uses the values 0 to 127 for its tokens, ASII uses 128 to 255, while 0 to 127 are the Ascii character set.

A Basic statement in Applesoft II is composed of five bytes, exclusive of any tokens, and is illustrated below in figure 3. Here is a sample program line, along with the hex bytes it is composed of.

Figure 3

100 REM			
07 30	64 00	B2	00
a.	b.	c.	d.

a. = Address of next Basic line.
b. = Line number.
c. = Token for "REM".
d. = End of line delimiter.

Neat text idea from "The APPLE CORPS".

Instead of:
```
100 PRINT"This message will appear on the
TV screen with broken words."
```

Try:
```
100 PRINT                               "
This message will appear on the TV
screen exactly as you see it here."
```

Up to 104 characters can be printed this way.

APPLESOFT Zero Page Useage

HEX LOCATION	USE
0-5	Jump instructions to continue in Applesoft. (OG for Applesoft is equivalent to Control C in Integer Basic.)
$A-$C	Location for USR( ) function jump instruction.
$D-$17	General purpose counters-flags for Applesoft.
$20-$4F	Apple II system monitor reserved locations.
$50-$61	General purpose pointers for Applesoft.
$67-68	Pointer to beginning of program. Normally set to $0801 for ROM version, or $3001 for RAM (cassette tape) version.
$69-$6A	Pointer to start of simple variable space. Also points to the end of the program plus 5, unless manually changed with the LOMEM: statement.
$6B-$6C	Pointer to the beginning of Array space.
$6D-$6E	Pointer to end of numeric storage in use.
$6F-$70	Pointer to start of string storage. Strings are stored from here to the end of memory.
$71-$72	General pointer.
$73-$74	Highest location in memory available to Applesoft plus one. Upon initial entry to Applesoft, is set to the end of memory available.
$75-$76	Current line number of line being executed.
$77-$78	"Old line number". Set up by a control-C, STOP or END statement. Gives line number that execution was interrupted at.
$79-$7A	"Old text pointer". Points to location in memory for statement to be executed next.
$7B-$7C	Current line number where DATA is being read from.
$7D-$7E	Points to absolute location in memory where DATA is being read from.
$7F-$80	Pointer to where input is coming from currently. Is set to $201 during an INPUT statement, or during a READ statement is set to the DATA in the program it is READing from.
$81-$82	Holds the last used variable name.
$83-$84	Pointer to the last used variable's value.
$85-9C	General useage.
$9D-$A3	Main floating point accumulator.
$a4	General use in floating point math routines.
$A5-$AB	Secondary floating point accumulator.
$aC-$B0	General useage flags-pointers.
$B1-$C8	CHRGET routine. Applesoft calls here every time it wants another character.
$B8-$B9	Pointer to last character obtained through the CHRGET routine.
$C9-$CD	Random number.
$D0-$DF	High resolution graphics scratch pointers.
$D8-$DF	ONERR pointers-scratch.
$E0-$E2	High-resolution graphics X and Y coordinates.
$E4	High-resolution graphics color byte.
$E5-$E7	General use for high resolution graphics.
$E8-$E9	Pointer to beginning of shape table.
$EA	Collision counter for high resolution graphics.
$F0-$F3	General use flags.
$F4-$F8	ONERR pointers.

ROUTINE to PRINT FREE BYTES
by Bob Huelsdonk

Only line 30001 is required for less than 32K of memory. The first GOTO 30000 shows result with >32K of memory. The second GOTO 30000 shows the result with <32K of memory.

```
30000 IF PEEK (203)>128 THEN 30002

30001 PRINT PEEK (202)+ PEEK (203
      )*256- PEEK (204)- PEEK (205
      )*256;" BYTES FREE": END
30002 PRINT 32767-( PEEK (204)+ PEEK
      (205)*256);" BYTES + "; PEEK
      (202)+( PEEK (203)-128)*256
      +1;" BYTES FREE": END


>GOTO30000
30719 BYTES + 16226 BYTES FREE


>GOTO30000
27793 BYTES FREE
```

APPLE II INTEGER BASIC INTERPRETATION OF MEMORY

LEAST SIGNIFICANT DIGIT

MSD \ LSD	0	1	2	3	4	5	6	7	8	9	A	B	C	D	E	F
0	HIMEM:	END OF STMT	▬	:	LOAD	SAVE	CON	RUN	RUN	DEL	,	NEW	CLR	AUTO	,	MAN
1	HIMEM: LOMEM:	+	+	-	*	/	=	#	>=	>	<=	<>	<	AND	OR	MOD
2	<	(	(	,	THEN	THEN	,	,	,,	,,	(	,!	!	!	PEEK	RND
3	SGN	ABS	PDL	RNDX	(	+	-	NOT	(	=	#	LEN(	ASC(	SCRN(	,	(
4	$	$	(	,	,	,	,,	,,	,	,	,	TEXT	GR	CALL	DIM	QIM
5	TAB	END	INPUT	INPUT	INPUT	FOR	=	TO	STEP	NEXT	,	RETURN	GOSUB	REM	LET	GOTO
6	IF	PRINT	PRINT	PRINT	POKE	,	COLOR=	PLOT	,	HLIN	,	AT	VLIN	,	AT	VTAB
7	=	=	)	)	,	,	LIST	POP	NODSP	NODSP	NOTRACE	DSP	DSP	TRACE	PR#	IN#
8	NUL	SOH	STX	ETX	EOT	ENQ	ACK	BEL	BS	HT	LF	VT	FF	CR	SO	SI
9	DLE	DC1	DC2	DC3	DC4	NAK	SYN	ETB	CAN	EM	SUB	ESC	FS	GS	RS	US
A	SP	!	"	#	$	%	&	'	(	)	*	+	,	-	.	/
B	0	1	2	3	4	5	6	7	8	9	:	;	<	=	>	?
C	@	A	B	C	D	E	F	G	H	I	J	K	L	M	N	O
D	P	Q	R	S	T	U	V	W	X	Y	Z	[	\	]	↑	←
E	`	a	b	c	d	e	f	g	h	i	j	k	l	m	n	o
F	p	q	r	s	t	u	v	w	x	y	z	{	|	}	~	del

ASCII EQUIV: 0 1 2 3 4 5 6 7

TOKENS — ASCII CHAR. & CONTROLS

MOST SIGNIFICANT DIGIT

VAL GOLDING + DON WILLIAMS 3-27-78

NOTE: Rows E+F will be output as upper case to Apple II Video Monitor

POINTERS & TOKENS FIGURE 2

LEAST SIGNIFICANT DIGIT

MSD	0	1	2	3	4	5	6	7	8	9	A	B	C	D	E	F	Decimal
8	END	FOR	NEXT	DATA	INPUT	DEL	DIM	READ	GR	TEXT	PR#	IN#	CALL	PLOT	HLIN	VLIN	128-143
9	HGR2	HGR	HCOLOR=	HPLOT	DRAW	XDRAW	HTAB	HOME	ROT=	SCALE=	SHLOAD	TRACE	NOTRACE	NORMAL	INVERSE	FLASH	144-159
A	COLOR=	POP	VTAB	HIMEM:	LOMEM:	ONERR	RESUME	RECALL	STORE	SPEED=	LET	GOTO	RUN	IF	RESTORE	&	160-175
B	GOSUB	RETURN	REM	STOP	ON	WAIT	LOAD	SAVE	DEF	POKE	PRINT	CONT	LIST	CLEAR	GET	NEW	176-191
C	TAB	TO	FN	SPC(	THEN	AT	NOT	STEP	+	-	*	/	^	AND	OR	>	192-207
D	=	<	SGN	INT	ABS	USR	FRE	SCRN(	PDL	POS	SQR	RND	LOG	EXP	COS	SIN	208-223
E	TAN	ATN	PEEK	LEN	STR$	VAL	ASC	CHR$	LEFT$	RIGHT$	MID$		SYNTAX	RETURN WITHOUT GOSUB	OUT OF DATA	ILLEGAL QUANTITY	224-239
F	OVERFLOW	OUT OF MEMORY	UNDEF'D STATEMENT	BAD SUBSCRIPT	REDIM'D ARRAY	DIVISION BY ZERO	ILLEGAL DIRECT	TYPE MISMATCH	STRING TOO LONG	FORMULA TOO COMPLEX	CAN'T CONTINUE	UNDEF'D FUNCTION	ERROR	(	(	(	240-255

APPLESOFT II TOKENS   Van Golding 05.28.78

NOTE: Values 00 to 7F (0 to 127 decimal) are used by the standard Ascii character set. As in Integer Basic, Apple II outputs last two rows (60-7F) as upper case.

This table is a complement to "Applesoft II Pointers and Tokens and should be saved as a permanent reference chart.

Memory Map — Apple II with APPLESOFT BASIC LOADED

MEMORY RANGE*   DESCRIPTION

Ø.1FF   Program work space; not available to user.

2ØØ.2FF   Keyboard character buffer.

3ØØ.3FF   Available to user for short machine language
                      programs.

4ØØ.7FF   Screen display area for text or color graphics.

8ØØ. 2FFF   APPLESOFT BASIC compiler. (Cassette Tape Version)

8ØØ.XXX   User Program (ROM version - A2B0009X installed) where
                      XXX is maximum available RAM memory

2000.3FFF   High Resolution Graphics Display page 1. May be
                      used by ROM (A2B0009X) version of Applesoft II only.

3000.XXX   User program (Cassette Tape Version) and variables
                      where XXX is maximum available RAM memory to be used
                      by APPLESOFT. This is either total system RAM
                      memory or less if the user is reserving part of
                      high memory for machine language routines.

4000.5FFF   High resolution graphics display page 2.

CØØØ.CFFF   Hardware I/O Addresses.

DØØØ.DFFF   Future ROM expansion

DØØØ.F7FF   Applesoft II ROM version with select switch "ON".

EØØØ.F7FF   Apple Integer BASIC

F8ØØ.FFFF   Apple System Monitor

LOADING MACHINE LANGUAGE AS PART OF A BASIC PROGRAM

from Contact No. 1, May, 1978

Often we want to include machine language data inside a Basic program. Apple Basic loads programs into memory with the highest program line at the highest RAM location (HIMEM) Preceeding lines are located lower and lower in RAM. The beginning of the program is at PP, an address which is held in memory locations CA and CB (hexadecimal) or 202 and 203, decimal. When you type SAVE, the computer transfers to tape everything between PP and HIMEM. Thus, to tuck machine language into your program so it can be loaded like Basic, it is merely necessary to move the PP down below the beginning of the extra code, put in two POKES to reset the pointer before running the program, and type SAVE. Later, you will be able to LOAD the whole thing just as if it were all Basic. Just follow these steps:

1. Get the Basic program into memory, exactly the way you want it. If you make any changes, you must redo steps 2 and 6.
2. In the command mode, type PRINT PEEK(202),PEEK(203) and write down the results. Call them m and n, respectively.
3. Load your machine language code into memory using the monitor load capability. This will put the machine language program into memory below the beginning of the basic program, starting at hexadecimal address xxxx.
4. Take the starting address of the machine language program and divide it into two parts: xx:xx. Convert each pair of digits from hex to decimal values: a & b, corresponding to the left and right xx pairs, respectively. Write them down.
5. Now enter the Basic command mode and type, POKE 202, b-1 (value b from step 4, above). POKE 203, a (value a from step 4, above). POKE 204,00; POKE 205,8
6. You have now moved the pointers down below your machine language program, and must insert code to move them back again when the program is run. To do that, type: 0 POKE 202,m; POKE 203,n; GOTO a   where m and n are the values from step 2 and a is the first line number in your Basic program. That line number can be 0.. it will not be erased by the above entry.
7. Now you're done! Don't try to list your program because before it runs, all you will see is a meaningless set of numbers and symbols. Just type SAVE (before running the program) and it will all go on to tape. Later a LOAD command will bring it all back in.

CAUTION !

Once you have RUN such a program, you cannot SAVE it, for the pointers will have been moved. You can only copy a program like this before it has been RUN.

A PATCH FOR DOUBLE LOOPS
BY BOB HUELSDONK

WHEN INPUTTING TO A DOUBLE LOOP BY ROW, THEN JUMPING OUT TO A DOUBLE LOOP TO TOTAL BY COLUMN, IT IS NECESSARY TO REVERSE THE SUBSCRIPT ORDER.

THIS WILL NOT WORK IN APPLESOFT BECAUSE THE RIGHT COUNTERS DO NOT RESET. THE FOLLOWING SIMPLE EXAMPLE WILL DEMONSTRATE:

```
80   PRINT " INPUT '-1' TO TERMINATE
     INPUTS"
100  FOR R = 1 TO 3
120  FOR C = 1 TO 3
140  INPUT A(R,C)
160  IF A(R,C) = - 1 THEN 300
180  NEXT C
200  NEXT R
300  FOR C = 1 TO 3
320  FOR R = 1 TO 3
340  PRINT A(R,C)
360  NEXT R
380  NEXT C
```

IF THE FOLLOWING CHANGES ARE MADE THIS PROBLEM IS OVERCOME?

```
160  IF A(R,C) = -1 THEN 250
250  FOR R=0 TO 0: NEXT R
```

THE EMPTY 'R' LOOP RESETS THE COUNTER.

EDITING in INTEGER or APPLESOFT

Reprinted from the April, 1978 Call -Apple. used by permission!

Here are two tools that will help speed up your program editing: First, to avoid those long end of line gaps in PRINT or REM statements, first clear your screen with a CALL -936. Then, POKE 33,33. Finally list the program lines you want to work on and, presto, they are all scrunched up. You have just reset the right window of your display, and those gaps have disappeared like magic! To return to normal, just type TEXT and hit return.

Have you ever found you needed to insert a word in your program statement, but there was no room? The easiest way to do that is with the escape keys, A, B, C and D. To insert a word, use escape D to go above the line, escape C to return to the line, and escape B to back up to where you left off. Unlike the forward and reverse arrow keys, the escape keys do not copy when you trace over characters.

The Program that Apple Said "Couldn't be Written" !!!
by Ron Aldrich

The Aldrich brothers strike again!. Remember, folks, you read it first in Call -Apple. "Convert", by Ron Aldrich, using the disk, will create a text file from an Integer Basic program listing, call Applesoft, then read the file into Applesoft and presto, your program has been converted! After conversion, list it out and note all lines that need to be changed to conform to the Applesoft format. This means that the Integer commands that are not compatible with Applesoft must be changed. For example: TAB must be changed to HTAB and commas in input statements must be changed to semicolons, etc.

```
0 REM "CONVERT" BY RON ALDRICH

1 REM PROGRAM LOADS INTEGER BASIC PROGRA
  M FROM DISK, SAVES TO A TEXT FILE ON D
  ISK
2 REM THEN EXECUTES THAT FILE IN APPLESO
  FT II
3 REM SOME COMMANDS WHICH ARE LEGAL IN I
  NTEGER BASIC WILL NOT WORK IN APPLESOF
  T II (TAB,INPUT...)

10 POKE 76, PEEK (202): POKE 77, PEEK
   (203)
20 DIM A$(35):D$="": REM  D$="(CTRL) D"
30 PRINT D$;"NOMON C,I,O"
40 TEXT : CALL -936: VTAB 3: PRINT "A.P.P
   .L.E.  PRESENTS:": PRINT : PRINT
   "APPLE INTEGER BASIC - APPLESOFT II"
   : PRINT "CONVERSION PROGRAM"
50 PRINT : PRINT : INPUT "PROGRAM TO BE C
   ONVERTED ?",A$
60 PRINT D$;"LOAD ";A$
65 PRINT D$
70 POKE 33,33
80 PRINT D$;"OPEN ";A$;"FILE": PRINT
   D$;"WRITE ";A$;"FILE"
90 LIST
100 PRINT D$;"CLOSE ";A$;"FILE"
105 PRINT D$
110 PRINT D$;"OPEN I-A FILE": PRINT D$
    ;"WRITE I-A FILE": PRINT "FP": PRINT
    "EXEC ";A$;"FILE"
120 PRINT D$;"CLOSE I-A FILE": PRINT
    D$;"EXEC I-A FILE"
130 END
       WELL, RANDY?
```

APPENDING APPLESOFT by Val Golding

Here are simple routines that will allow you to append programs in both version of Applesoft. While appending can be done underprogram control in Ap.II, it is really simpler to do it without. The routines are the same in both versions; only the pointers have been changed (to protect the innocent!). A word of caution: Applesoft programs store in memory just the opposite of Integer Basic, i.e., from the bottom up. Therefore, the first program appended should be the one with the lowest line numbers. You will get an error message in Ap.I, which should be disregarded. The secret is in changing the values of the pointers (106 & 107 in Ap. I) or (103 & 104) in Ap. II). This "hides" the first program while the second is being loaded. To do this, these pointers must be set to equal the value of the program pointer, less 2. In Ap.I the PP is 112 & 113; in Ap II it is 109 & 110. Here is the routine; just use the proper pointers for version I or II.

```
POKE 103, (PEEK(109)-2)
POKE 104,  PEEK(110)
LOAD
POKE 103, 1:POKE 104, 48 (for Ap. II)
POKE 106, 1:POKE 107, 42 (for Ap. I)
```

Do not attempt to list, run, renumber, etc. until all of the routine has been completed or it will blow your Applesoft.

CONVERTING APPLESOFT I TO II

Load the converter program in Integer Basic and Run. The program will instruct you when to load your Applesoft I program when conversion is complete and you have resaved your Applesoft I program, load it into Applesoft II and list. You will then need to manually correct commands to the new format, i.e., PLTG becomes GR.

Note Illegal line 1: enter manually

```
0 TEXT : CALL -936: VTAB 3: PRINT
  "APPLESOFT CONVERSION PROGRAM:"

1 LOMEM:2048
2 PRINT "
          CONVERTS OLD APPLESOFT PR
  OGRAMS TO": PRINT "APPLESOFT ][
  FORMAT"
3 PRINT "
          COPYRIGHT 1978 APPLE COMP
  UTER, INC.
                  "
4 PRINT "


          ": POKE 34,10
5 PRINT "WAS PROGRAM WRITTEN IN OP
  TION 1 OR": PRINT "OPTION 2?
                                "
  : PRINT "OPTION 1: GRAPHICS COMM
  ANDS WITHOUT"
6 PRINT "             LET OR REM STA
  TEMENTS": PRINT "
               OPTION 2: LET A
  ND REM STATEMENTS BUT NO
       GRAPHICS."
7 INPUT "OPTION #",O: IF O<>1
  AND O<>2 THEN 7
10 CALL -936: PRINT "PUT APPLESOFT
   PROGRAM TAPE IN RECORDER,":
   POKE 60,Z: POKE 61,Z: POKE
   62,2: POKE 63,Z:F=1536:B=4096

20 INPUT "PRESS THE PLAY BUTTON, TH
   EN HIT RETURN",A$: CALL -259

25 IF PEEK (1)<123 THEN 30: PRINT
   "

   TAPE READ ERROR!": PRINT "TRY R
   E-ADJUSTING VOLUME CONTROLS ON T
   APEPLAYER, THEN RE-RUN THIS PROG
   RAM"
30 POKE 60,Z: POKE 61,16:E= PEEK
   (Z)+ PEEK (1)*256-6657: POKE
   62:E MOD 256: POKE 63,E/256
   : CALL -259
35 CALL -936: PRINT "


                 CONVERTING..."

40 IF B>=E THEN 1000:A= PEEK (
   B)+F MOD 256: POKE B,A MOD
   256: POKE B+1, PEEK (B+1)+F/
   256+(A>255)
```

```
50 FOR B=B+4 TO B+999:T= PEEK
   (B): IF T<133 THEN 250: IF
   T<>135 AND T<>142 OR O=2 THEN
   200:C=B
55 IF T<>142 THEN 60:T=137: GOTO
   250
60 C=C+1:U= PEEK (C): IF U=32 THEN
   60: IF U=67 OR U=71 OR U=72
   OR U=80 OR U=86 THEN GOTO
   U: PRINT "BAD STATEMENT IN PROGR
   AM": GOTO 250
67 T=160: GOTO 90
71 T=136: GOTO 90
72 T=142: GOTO 87
80 T=141: GOTO 90
86 T=143
87 CC=Z:D=B
88 D=D+1: IF PEEK (D)<>44 AND
   PEEK (D)<>58 AND PEEK (D) THEN
   88: IF PEEK (D)=44 THEN 89:
   PRINT "BAD STATEMENT IN PROGRAM
   !": GOTO 250
89 CC=CC+1: IF CC=1 THEN 88: POKE
   D,197
90 POKE C,32: GOTO 250
199 REM :MAP OLD TOKENS TO NEW
200 IF T>195 THEN 250:T=T+1+(T>
    134)*34+(T>139)+(T>160)+(T>
    177)*2
250 POKE B,T: IF B/500*500=B THEN
    PRINT "STILL CONVERTING!"
251 IF T<>0 THEN NEXT B:B=B+1: GOTO
    40
878 CC=Z:D=C
1000 CALL -936: POKE 60,Z: POKE
     61,Z: POKE 62,2: POKE 63,Z:
     PRINT "DONE!
                  ": INPUT "START REC
     ORDING, THEN HIT 'RETURN'",
     A$
1001 POKE E-2,Z: POKE E-1,Z: POKE
     E,Z
1005 D=E-4096: POKE Z,D MOD 256:
     POKE 1,D/256: POKE 2,Z: CALL
     -307
1010 POKE 60,Z: POKE 61,16: POKE
     62,E MOD 256: POKE 63,E/256
     : CALL -307
1020 PRINT "O.K.

                  ": PRINT "THE TAPE JU
     ST RECORDED CAN NOW BE LOADED IN
     TO APPLESOFT ][.": END
```

BULLETIN: Our library now has a LCOS
(Limited Cassette Operating System)

LINKAGE ROUTINES
for the Apple II Integer Basic
FLOATING POINT PACKAGE

by   DON WILLIAMS

Floating point numbers are treated by the Apple II Rom Routines as four bytes represented in Figure 1, below:

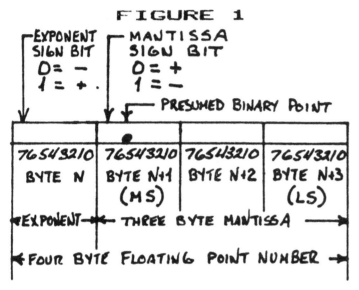

FIGURE 1

with the number being represented as in scientific notation

as: MANTISSA $\times 2^{(exponent)}$

The exponent byte is biased by 80 hex and represents the number of implied binary point moves to the right (80-FF) or to the left (00-7F) of the binary point. For example:

FIGURE 2 / FIGURE 3
EXPONENTS / FLOATING POINT NUMBERS

EXPONENTS	FLOATING POINT NUMBERS	
00 IS -128	83 50 00 00	10.
01 IS -127	00 40 00 00	1.
02 IS -126	7C 66 66 66	.1
:	00 00 00 00	0.0
7F IS -1	7C 49 99 9A	-.1
80 IS 0	7F 80 00 00	-1.0
81 IS +1	83 B0 00 00	-10.0
:	80 60 00 00	1.5
FF IS 127	80 70 00 00	1.75

The three byte mantissa (or fractional part of the number) is standard two's complement notation with the sign bit in the most significant (MS) bit (bit 7) of the high order byte. The assumed binary point is between bits 6 and 5 of the same byte. In this representation, a properly normalized number will have a mantissa whose absolute value is be-

tween 1 and 2. A properly normalized number will have the most significant two bits unequal:

    01.XXXXXX positive mantissa (MS) byte
    10.XXXXXX negative mantissa (MS) byte

The programs documented here will build these numbers from Integer Basic numbers and call the floating point routines.

There are several parts to the floating point linkage routines you will have to understand in order to successfully use them. First I will discuss what memory locations are used, and then the several Basic subroutines that use them.

MEMORY
LOCATION

0   - This location will be incremented if an error occurs in the floating point routines (such as $2^{127} \times 2^{127}$)

1   - This location will contain the floating point op code (operation).

OP
CODE   FIGURE 4

OP CODE			
0 = FIX		R(A) →	R(C)
1 = FLOAT		R(A) →	R(C)
2 = ADD	R(B) + R(A) →	R(C)
3 = SUBTRACT	R(B) - R(A) →	R(C)
4 = MULTIPLY	R(B) * R(A) →	R(C)
5 = DIVIDE	R(B) / R(A) →	R(C)
6 = ABS VALUE	R(A) →	R(C)
7 = COMPLIMENT	R(B) - R(A) →	R(C)
8 = SWAP	R(A) →	R(C)

2,3   - These locations contain the address of the floating point array (i.e. REAL(127) or R(127))

4,5   - These locations contain the address of the first operands index (i.e., A)

6,7   - These locations contain the address of the second operands index (i.e., B)

8,9   - These locations contain the address of the results index (i.e., C)

A,1F   - These locations are used for scratch storage.

300-376 - These locations contain the machine language linkage programs.

In the description of the various program segments, I will proceed in a logical, rather than sequential, manner.

BASIC LINE   PURPOSE
    400   - "Float": Store the value of "INT" into the Real array at location "A"

700-1500	"Fix": Convert the value in the Real array at location "C" into its integer and fractional parts in "INT" and "FRAC"
4500-4900	Set up the pointer (memory 0-9)
3800	Calculate the address where the next variable defined will be stored.
4300	Poke an address into memory
5100	Build the floating point number 10000. (This is used in FIX and FLOAT)
5300-5400	Build the floating point number .5 (This is used in FIX)
5700-5800	Float (I) => Real (B). Note B=4 & C=4.
6000-6100	Float (J) => Real (A). Note A=0 & C=0.
6400	Real (B) (Op) Real (A) -> Real (Q).
6450	SQRT (Real (Q)) => TEMP @ Real (240).
450	Print the floating value in INT and FRAC.
205-260	Calculate the square root of the number in Real (A).

Since the program segment to calculate the square root is the least clear, I will try to delineate its operation. The derivation of the Newton iteration solution for square root is as follows:

FIGURE 5

$$\sqrt{A} = C$$
$$A = C^2$$
$$C^2 - A = 0$$
$$IF\ C_N = ?$$
$$THEN\ C_{(N+1)} = \frac{C + (\frac{A}{C_N})}{2}$$

A flow chart outlining the square root segment is shown as figure 6 in column 2.

THE SAGA of OLD No. 8

(Or what else could possibly go wrong ???)

"Program 8 won't load" was the complaint we heard in droves, when Library Pak 1B was first released. Unfortunately, by that time, we had released over 30 copies of that infamous pak. So, we decided, we would make that program the first program on the soon-to-be-released pak 2. This would be a way to make amends without re-recording a large batch of tapes. But we had not taken into account the whims of the computer gods. For lo and behold, on Library Pak 2, there came to be a duplication of Color Gamepak 2, and no Color Gamepak 1. So we are once again on our knees, begging for mercy!

This error occured on all copies of pak 2 numbered <48. If you still need old no. 8, then send a note and a self-addressed envelope and we'll make amends. Shameful, shameful!

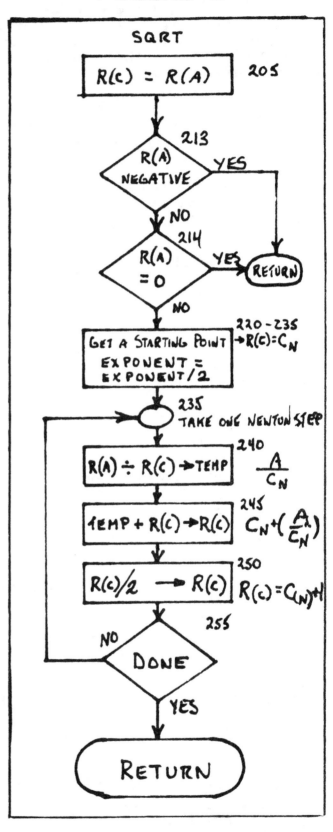

FIGURE 6

The "REAL" array can contain up to 64 floating point variables (The last three are used by FIX and FLOAT) indexes A,B & C represent bytes so that the first is 0, while the second is 4 and the I'th is (I-1)*4, so the value of user indexes can range from 0-240 in steps of 4.

The machine language routines reside in Basic lines 7200 to 7500 and will be placed in memory by a small Basic routine in lines 3200-3600. A GOSUB 7200 will place the program into memory, ready to use.

As for size and speed, the Basic program occupies 1193 bytes of memory and runs at the following rates:

FIGURE 7

	TIME IN MILLISECS		AVG #/SEC	INT. OPS/SEC
	MIN	MAX		
FIX	5.7	5.8	174	-
FLOAT	4.7	4.7	213	-
ADD	5.1	17.9	87	500
SUBTRACT	5.3	17.9	86	500
MULTIPLY	7.1	7.3	139	400
DIVIDE	8.0	9.1	117	333
ABS VALUE	4.7	4.7	213	-
COMPLIMENT	4.7	4.7	213	-
SWAP	4.7	4.7	213	-

Even though these times are large in comparison with the equivalent integer operations, it should be remembered that Basic spends much more time keeping track of what it's doing than doing it.

```
90 REM   "INTEGER BASIC FLOATING POI
   NT LINKAGE ROUTINES"

100 REM   WRITTEN BY DON WILLIAMS 2/7
    8
200 GOTO 4400
204 REM   REAL(C) = SQRT(REAL(A))
205 REAL(C/2)=REAL(A/2):REAL(C/
    2+1)=REAL(A/2+1)
210 TA=A:TB=B:TC=C
213 IF PEEK (RL+A+1)>127 THEN RETURN

214 IF REAL(A/2)=0 THEN RETURN

215 K= PEEK (RL+C)
220 IF K>128 THEN K=(K-128)/2+128

225 IF K<128 THEN K=128-(128-K)
    /2
230 POKE RL+C,K
```

```
235 FOR KK=1 TO 6
240 B=TA:A=TC:C=248: POKE 1,5: CALL
    790
245 B=248:C=TC: POKE 1,2: CALL
    790
250 POKE RL+C, PEEK (RL+C)-1
255 NEXT KK
260 A=TA:B=TB:C=TC: RETURN
300 REM   REAL(A) = FLOAT (INT)
400 REAL(A/2)=INT: POKE RL+A+2,
    PEEK (RL+A): POKE RL+A+3,0
    : RETURN
450 PRINT INT;: IF PEEK (36)>( PEEK
    (33)-6) THEN PRINT : PRINT
    FRAC+10000;:L= PEEK (36): TAB
    L-4: PRINT ".";: TAB L+3: RETURN

500 REM   INT = IFIX (REAL(C))
600 REM   FRAC = (REAL(C) - INT) * 10
    000
700 REAL(124)=REAL(C/2):REAL(125
    )=REAL(C/2+1):TA=A:TB=B:TC=
    C
800 B=C: POKE 1,0:A=C: CALL 790

900 POKE RL+C, PEEK (RL+C+2):INT=
    REAL(C/2): POKE RL+C+3,0: POKE
    1,1: CALL 790
1000 B=248: POKE 1,3: CALL 790
1100 B=252: POKE 1,4: CALL 790
1200 B=244: POKE 1,2: CALL 790
1300 POKE 1,0: CALL 790
1400 POKE RL+C, PEEK (RL+C+2):FRAC=
     REAL(C/2):A=TA:B=TB:C=TC
1500 IF FRAC>=0 THEN RETURN :FRAC=
     0:INT=-1: RETURN
```

NIGHTMARE GAMEPAK

In another maddening example of shoddy craftsmanship, here are some patches to be made in Nightmare Gamepak for copies number <48. Load the program, make changes as shown below, and resave it.

```
Renumber line 2392 to 2389 and delete 2392
Renumber line 2394 to 2391 and delete 2394
Correct line 2106 to read GOTO 2496
Line 2216 change END to GOTO 2496
Add line 2496 FOR I=1 TO 2500:GOTO 20160:
     NEXT I:
```

```
3200  REM    SUBROUTINE TO STORE THE HE
      X DATA IN STRING S$ INTO MEMORY
      AT LOCATON L
3300  FOR I=1 TO LEN(S$) STEP 2
3400  J= ASC(S$(I))-176: IF J>9 THEN
      J=J-7
3500  K= ASC(S$(I+1))-176: IF K>9
      THEN K=K-7
3600  POKE L,J*16+K:L=L+1: NEXT I:
      RETURN
3800  L= PEEK (204)+ PEEK (205)*256
      +3+ LEN(V$): RETURN
4300  GOSUB 3800: POKE IA,L MOD 256
      : POKE IA+1,L/256: RETURN
4400  DIM V$(10):V$="S$": GOSUB 3800
      : DIM S$(255):SL=L: GOSUB 7200

4500  REM   DEFINE THE F.P. POINTERS
4600  V$="REAL":IA=2: GOSUB 4300:
      DIM REAL(127):RL=L: POKE 0
      ,0
4700  V$="A":IA=4: GOSUB 4300:A=0

4800  V$="B":IA=6: GOSUB 4300:B=4

4900  V$="C":IA=8: GOSUB 4300:C=8

5000  REM   REAL(126,127) = 10000.
5100  INT=10000: GOSUB 400:C=252:
      POKE 1,1: CALL 790
5200  REM   REAL(122,123) = 1./2.
5300  INT=5000: GOSUB 400:C=244: POKE
      1,1: CALL 790
5400  B=244:A=252: POKE 1,5: CALL
      790
5500  B=4:A=0
5600  FOR I=1 TO 10
5650  REM   FLOAT I==> REAL(1)
5700  INT=I: GOSUB 400
5800  C=4: POKE 1,1: CALL 790
5900  FOR J=1 TO 10
5950  REM   FLOAT J==> REAL(0)
6000  INT=J: GOSUB 400
6100  C=0: POKE 1,1: CALL 790
6200  PRINT I;"@";J;"=",
6300  FOR Q=2 TO 7
6350  REM   R(4) (+) R(0) ==> R(Q)
6400  C=(Q+1)*4: POKE 1,Q: CALL 790
```

```
6425  REM   SQRT(R(Q)) ==> TEMP
6450  A=C:C=240: GOSUB 205:C=A
6500  GOSUB 700: GOSUB 450
6550  C=240: GOSUB 700: GOSUB 450

6600  A=0: NEXT Q: PRINT
6700  NEXT J
6800  IF PEEK (-16384)<128 THEN 6800

6900  POKE -16368,0
7000  NEXT I
7100  END
7200  L=768: REM     300-376      FLOATING
       POINT LINKAGE ROUTINE
7300  S$="186502850AA50369008508608A003
      B10A910C8810F960A0F4B90000991CFF
      C8D0F7EAEAEAA2F4860C840DB1062000
      03200C03": GOSUB 3300
7400  S$="A9F88850CA000B104200003200C03
      206003A000B108200003A003B10C910A
      8810F9A0F4B91CFF990000C8D0F760EA
      A9F6A401": GOSUB 3300
7500  S$="F002A9F44BB96E0348603F506D67
      BBB131A340": GOSUB 3300: RETURN
```

APPLESOFT   TONE   SUBROUTINES

by John B. Cook

The handy tone subroutines from the the red Apple II
Reference Manual are a nice addition to many programs. Unfortunately, they won't run in Applesoft Basic. As listed
in the manual, they are in the wrong place in memory. They
will work, however, if relocated as listed below:

MACHINE LANGUAGE PROGRAM

```
0308-    FF                ???
0309-    FF                ???
030A-    AD 30 C0    LDA    $C030
030D-    88          DEY
030E-    D0 05       BNE    $0315
0310-    CE 09 03    DEC    $0309
0313-    F0 09       BEQ    $031E
0315-    CA          DEX
0316-    D0 F5       BNE    $030D
0318-    AE 08 03    LDX    $0308
031B-    4C 0A 03    JMP    $030A
031E-    60          RTS
```

```
31000 REM    BASIC "POKES"


32000 POKE 776,255: POKE 777,255:
      POKE 778,173: POKE 779,48:
      POKE 780,192: POKE 781,136
    : POKE 782,208: POKE 783,5:
      POKE 784,206: POKE 785,9: POKE
    786,3: POKE 787,240
32010 POKE 788,9: POKE 789,202: POKE
      790,208: POKE 791,245: POKE
      792,174: POKE 793,8: POKE 794
    ,3: POKE 795,76: POKE 796,10
    : POKE 797,3: POKE 798,96: RETURN

32100 REM    GOSUB


  25 POKE 776,P: POKE 777,D: CALL
     778: RETURN : REM  SET PITCH & D
     URATION


32767 REM  GOSUB 32000 ONCE AT BEGINNI
      NG OF PROGRAM THEN GOSUB 25 ANYW
      HERE IN PROGRAM
```

6502 PROGRAM EXCHANGE

Apple II users can now run an extended version of the
high-level language FOCAL* (*DEC trademark). FCL65E is now
available in Apple II cassette form for $25 from the 6502
Program Exchange, 2920 Moana, Reno, Nv. 89509. Manuals and
sorce listings are also available at additional cost.   Programs in FOCAL for Apple are also available.

Apple PASCAL is under development in southern California and a few copies have been released for sale. When details are available, you will read about it in Call -Apple.
Rumors are also rampant about an Apple version of FORTH. If
anyone can supply information about this, we would be great-
ful.

"ALAS, POOR BASIC, I KNEW IT WELL!"

THE PICTURE OF SHAKESPEARE, ABOVE, IS FROM THE APPLE SOFT-
WARE BANK, AND WAS PRINTED ON THE INTEGRAL DATA PRINTER.

SPACE FOR NOTES

```
                    ****************************
                    *                          *
                    *      SIMPLE TONES        *
                    *   A DEMONSTRATION FOR    *
                    *     EXTENSIONS TO        *
                    *     APPLESOFT-II         *
                    *                          *
                    *    SEPTEMBER, 1978       *
                    *                          *
                    *      R. WIGGINTON        *
                    ****************************
                    *
                    * SIMPLE TONE PROGRAM FOR APPLESOFT-II
                    * INSIDE THE APPLESOFT PROGRAM:
                    *  &T <NOTE>,<DURATION>
                    * THIS MUSIC ROUTINE IS NOT CALIBRATED TO ANY SCALE
                    * WHATSOEVER.
                    *
                    CHRGET     EQU     $00B1
                    CHRGOT     EQU     $00B7
                    SPKR       EQU     $C030
                    GETBYT     EQU     $E6F8
                    SNERR      EQU     $DEC9
                    WAIT       EQU     $FCA8
                               ORG     $0300
0300 C9 54         SIMTON     CMP     #$54 ; 'T' FOR TONE?
0302 D0 0F                    BNE     GIVERR ;IF NOT, GIVE A SYNTAX ERROR
0304 20 B1 00                 JSR     CHRGET ;GO OVER THE 'T'
0307 20 F8 E6                 JSR     GETBYT ;AND GET A VALUE FROM 0-255 FOR THE
030A 8A                       TXA     ;PRESERVE                          NOTE
030B 48                       PHA
030C 20 B7 00                 JSR     CHRGOT ; IS IT A COMMA NEXT?
030F C9 2C                    CMP     #$2C
0311 F0 03                    BEQ     OK
0313 4C C9 DE     GIVERR      JMP     SNERR ;NO IT WASN'T A COMMA, BLOW HIM AWAY.
0316 20 B1 00     OK          JSR     CHRGET ;EAT THE COMMA.
0319 20 F8 E6                 JSR     GETBYT ;NOW GET THE LENGTH OF THE NOTE.
                    *
                    * NOW PLAY THE NOTE.
                    *
031C 68           PLAY        PLA     ;GET NOTE FROM STACK.
031D 48                       PHA     ;COPY BACK ONTO THE STACK
031E 20 A8 FC                 JSR     WAIT ;DELAY BEFORE CLICKING SPEAKER AGAIN
0321 AD 30 C0                 LDA     SPKR ;CLICK THE SPEAKER.
0324 CA                       DEX
0325 D0 F5                    BNE     PLAY ;KEEP PLAYING.
0327 68                       PLA     ;CLEAR UP STACK.
0328 60                       RTS     ;GO BACK INTO APPLESOFT.
                    *
                    * APPLESOFT EXTENSION LINK:
                    *
                               ORG     $3F5
03F5 4C 00 03     EXTLOC      JMP     SIMTON
```

SAVE MEMORY ON A STRING
by Don Williams

One of the minor deficiencies in Apple Integer Basic is the omission of the Data statement. In search of a remedy for this, I wrote a program to save memory in a Basic string assignment. This is listed as program lines 1020 through 1190.

Upon embarking on the first routine, I quickly found a second ommission in the langauge; a way to store a non-string variable into a string, the remedy for which is shown as program lines 1250 through 1300. Finally, in the interest of completeness, a third routine, given as lines 1200 to 1240, stores the data back into memory.

Running the program that saves memory is fairly straightforward, and is self-prompting. The data to be saved is displayed on the screen, and after the prompt returns, just press the cursor right and repeat keys until you pass the end of the generated statement(s), then hit return. That line is now a part of your Basic program; repeat the procedure for subsequent lines.

Wherever logically in your program you want the same data loaded back into Memory, place a call to the first line generated by the program, and a return after the last line generated. After storing the program, if memory space is at a premium, just delete those lines.

The second routine, (lines 1250-1300), locates any predefined variable in memory, and can readily be interfaced with a tape read/write routine where data needs to move from program to program. (See Apple II Reference Manual, pages 34-43) I have been able to use this program to locate variables for use in an Integer Basic floating point routine, a very fast f.p. which will be published in the June issue. Program listing are in column two.

```
1020 REM SAVE MEMORY ON A STRING BY
     DON WILLIAMS, APRIL 1978
1030 DIM S$(255),V$(10)
1040 PRINT "ENTER STARTING ADDRESS,
     ENDING ADDRESS AND LINE NUMBER"
1050 INPUT IST,IND,STMT
1060 CALL -936:PRINT "ENTER LINES
     BELOW INTO PROGRAM"
1070 PRINT " ";STMT;" L= ";IST
1080 V$="S$*":GOSUB 1260:SL=L
1090 POKE SL,162
1100 K=1:FOR I=IST TO IND: N=PEEK(I):
     M=N/16:N=N-16*M
1110 IF M>9 THEN M=M+7:M=M+176
1120 IF N>9 THEN N=N+7:N=N+176
1130 POKE SL+K,M:POKE SL+K+1,N
1140 K=K+2:IF K<100 THEN 1170
1150 GOSUB 1190
1160 K=1
1170 NEXT I
1180 IF K#1 THEN GOSUB 1190:VTAB 1:
     TAB 1:END
1190 POKE SL+K,162:POKE SL+K+1,0:
     STMT=STMT+10:PRINT " ";STMT;
     " S$= ";S$;":GOSUB 1210:RETURN
1200 REM SUBROUTINE TO STORE THE
     HEX DATA IN STRING S$ INTO
     MEMORY AT LOCATION L
1210 FOR I=1 TO LEN(S$) STEP 2
1220 J=ASC(S$(I))-176:IF J>9 THEN
     J=J-7
1230 K=ASC(S$(I+1))-176:IF K>9
     THEN K=K-7
1240 POKE L,J*16+K:L=L+1:NEXT I:
     RETURN
1250 REM SUBROUTINE TO FIND STARTING
     ADDRESS FOR VARIABLE WHOSE NAME
     IS IN V$. L=ADDRESS OR -1
     IF UNDEFINED
1260 L=PEEK(74)+PEEK(75)*256-1: K=
     LEN(V$)-1: J=PEEK(204) +
     PEEK(205) * 256-1
1270 FOR I=1 TO K:IF ASC(V$(I))#
     PEEK(L+1) THEN 1290
1280 IF PEEK(L+K+1)>1 THEN
1290:L=L+K+4:RETURN
1290 FOR I=1 TO 100:IF PEEK(I+L)>1
     THEN NEXT I: I=L+I+1: L=PEEK(I)
     + PEEK(I+1) * 256-1
1300 IF L<J THEN 1270:L=L-1:RETURN
```

PEEKS, POKES and CALLS

Peeks, Pokes and Calls are among the powerful commands at your disposal. They permit you to wander through the passageways and corridors of your Apple's memory. RAM memory may be looked upon as a huge old-fashioned post office file cabinet, with 65,536 pigeon holes, which are actually memory "locations", numbered from 0 to 65535 (decimal) or from 0 to FFFF (hex). Each location is capable of holding one one byte (or unit) of data (information). A "byte" is a hexidecimal number with a value between 0 and FF (0 to 255, decimal).

Hexidecimal is a number base in which the unit column may have a value between 0 and 15. The numbers 10 to 15 are expressed as the letters A through F, thus F equals 15, while hex 10 equals 16. The dollar sign ($) is commonly used to indicate a hex number. In number systems, hex is known as base 16. Other number systems used in microcomputers are octal (base 8) and binary (base 2). Your Apple actually works in binary, but this is essentially an internal process that most users are unaware of.

Any hex number greater than FF must be stored in memory as two consecutive bytes, with the low order byte stored first. To convert a two byte hex number to decimal, we must do more than simply convert the hex values to decimal. For an example, let us take the hex number 7FFF (remembering that this will appear as FF7F (in reverse order) as you look at it in memory) and convert it to decimal. The procedure is always the same: the high order (second) byte is multiplied by 256 and the value of the low order (first) byte is added to the result. Therefore, 7F=127, 127*256=32512, and FF= 255, so 32512+255=32767. We have just converted 7FFF stored as two consecutive hex bytes of FF and 7F to their decimal equivalent of 32767! A working knowledge of hex is needed to put all the power of Apple at your beck and CALL.

The CALL command is to assembly (or machine) language what GOSUB is to Basic. Instead of saying GOSUB and specifying a Basic line number, you write a Call to a memory location. The effect is the same: you are asking Apple to execute a subroute, only in machine language instead of Basic.

POKE and PEEK are opposites, and aptly named. POKE is the command that allows you to store data in memory, perhaps for use at a later time. For example, a tone subroutine in Integer Basic may be located in hex locations 2 to 18. Locations $0 and $1 are to be used to store the values of the variables PITCH and DURATION, (commonly P & D. So a line in your program might read: 100 P=25: D=150: POKE 0,P: POKE 1,D: CALL 2

A PEEK command allows you to look inside the very core (pun intended) of your Apple and see what is stored there. Example: you want to know what your high mem is set at. The values of "HIMEM" are stored in decimal locations 76 and 77 (remember, this is a two byte figure), so you can use this simple algorhythm to find out:

PRINT PEEK (76) + PEEK (77) * 256

Incidently, these are called "pointers" because they "point" to where high memory actually is. Another example of useing the PEEK command is when you want the computer to "peek" at the keyboard to see if the user has typed a character or not. A common way to do this is as follows: Assume you are asking the user to type a Y or N to indicate yes or no. You could write it like this:

```
100 KEY = PEEK(-16384)
110 IF KEY < 128 THEN 110
120 IF KEY = 217 THEN 200
130 END
```

In Integer Basic, the "Ascii" character set has values between 128 and 255. If the variable "key" in our example is less than 128, it means no key has been typed, and the program has been sent back to read the keyboard again, until such time as the user actually types a character. 217 is the Ascii value for the character "Y".

RESURECTING a DEAD FP PROGRAM

Have you ever had an Applesoft II program "blow up" while you were working on it, only to find that you had not SAVEd it and could not remember the algorhythms you used? (They were probably based on the trial and error method, anyway), and it cost you a couple hours to recreate them?

Here is a short routine for Applesoft ROM that may help you recover your program. It requires that you be able to look into your memory and be able to identify the first two line numbers of the lost program. In addition, you must know the make-up of Applesoft Basic. It is as follows: The first two bytes are the address of the next line, and the next two bytes are the actual line number, stored low byte first. The last byte of a line is a "00" token, indicating the end of a line.

ROM Applesoft stores starting at decimal location 2049. On a disk reboot, the two locations that normally contain the address of the next line will have zeroes in them. The zeroes must be replaced with the correct next line address. Then you must estimate the length of the original program, and reset pointers as follows:

Say your program was about two K long. That is, approximately 2048 bytes. Add the program length to 2048 (start of memory), and divide by 256. (4096/256=16). Then poke your pointers (from the keyboard) as follows:

POKE 105,0:POKE 106,16:POKE 107,7:POKE 108,16: POKE 109,7:POKE 110,16: POKE 175,0:POKE 176,16:CALL 54514.

The pairs (107-8) and (109-10) must always be seven bytes more than the pairs (105-6) and (175-6). The CALL 54514 is a routine that helps you reassign the next line address pointers.

```
10 REM ROUTINE TO FORMAT DECIMAL
   NUMBERS ROUNDED OFF TO TWO
   PLACES AND RIGHT JUSTIFIED
        BY BOB HUELSDONK

15 REM 4/27/78

20 REM APPLE PUGETSOUND PROGRAM
   LIBRARY EXCHANGE
   6708 39TH AVE SW
   SEATTLE, WA 98136

70 FOR I = 1 TO 10: READ A:P = A:
   GOSUB 6000
75 PRINT P$: NEXT
80 END
90 DATA 56.2, 23456.1, 5, 1.186,
   345.70, 23, 678.01223,
   -99999.889, .2389, 789567
100 REM
110 REM 'A' WAS CHANGEO TO 'P'
120 REM TO KEEP THE SUBROUTINE
130 REM ANONYMOUS
140 REM WORKS FOR P<999999
150 REM BUT CAN BE INCREASED

6000 P$ = STR$(P)
6010 FOR J= 1 TO LEN (P$): IF MID$
     (P$,J,1) < > "." THEN NEXT
6015 IF J = LEN (PS) + 1 THEN P$
     = P$ + "."
6028 IF LEN (P8) < J + 2 THEN 6040
6025 IF VAL (MID$ (P$,J+3,1)) < 5
     THEN 6035
6030 P$ = MID$ (P$,1,J + 1) +
     RIGHT$ (STR$(VAL(MID$
     (P$,J+2,1)+1),1)
6035 P$ = MID$ (P$,1,J + 2)
6040 IF LEN ( LEFT$ (P$,J)) > = 7
     THEN 6050
6045 P$ =" " + P$: J=J+1: GOTO
     6040
6050 IF LEN (P$) > = 9 THEN 6060
6055 P$ = P$ +  "0":GOTO 6050
6060 RETURN
```

Input P may be substituted for 90 DATA above, and other minor modifications made to suit your program. Save routines like the above and append them to your programs.

```
10   REM ROUTINE TO FORMAT REMARKS
     LINES AND PRINT STATEMENTS
     IN APPLESOFT II
     BY VAL GOLDING   5-20-1978

20   REM APPLE PUGETSOUND PROGRAM
     LIBRARY EXCHANGE
     6708 39TH AVE SW
     SEATTLE, WA. 98136

90   HOME : VTAB 4
100  PRINT "THIS ROUTINE ALLOWS
     YOU TO FORMAT REM LINES AND
     PRINT STATEMENTS. DO NOT
     ENTER DATA IN THE SPACES.":
     PRINT
105  PRINT: PRINT: HTAB 8: PRINT
     "SELECT ONE:   ": PRINT:
     PRINT:HTAB 12:PRINT "REM ":
     " PRINT : HTAB 12: PRINT
     "PRINT ": INPUT "[";A$
110  IF A$ = "PRINT" THEN 180
130  HOME : VTAB 2
138  REM ENTER GROUPS OF 24
     DASHES AND 4 SPACES
140  PRINT "  000
     REM------------------------
     ------------------------
     ------------------------
     ------------------------
     ------------------------
     ------------------------"
150  IF PEEK (37) < 10 THEN 140
168  PRINT : PRINT " GOTO 130
     (FOR MORE LINES)"
170  VTAB ( PEEK (37) = -22):END
180  HOME: VTAB 2
188  REM ENTER 39 DASHES AND 1 SPACE
190  PRINT : PRINT "  000 ? '-----
     -------------------------------------
     -------------------------------------
     --- -------------------------------
     -------- ------------------------
     ------------- --------------------
     ------------------ ----------------
     ---------------------- '"
200  IF PEEK (37) < 18 THEN 190
210  PRINT : PRINT " GOTO 180
     (FOR MORE LINES)"
220  VTAB ( PEEK (37) + 19): END
```

```
LIST

100  PRINT
110  REM ROUTINE TO DISPLAY
     APPLESOFT PROGRAM TOKENS
     BY VAL GOLDING AND
     BOB HUELSDONK

120  REM APPLE PUGETSOUND PROGRAM
     LIBRARY EXCHANGE
     6708 39TH AVE SW
     SEATTLE, WA. 98136

180  D=1
200  HOME: A=1: B=128: C=12293
210  POKE C,B: LIST 100: VTAB
     ( PEEK (37) - 1)
220  IF D = 1 THEN GOSUB 700
230  IF D = 2 THEN GOSUB 522
240  VTAB (PEEK (37)): B=B+1:
     A=A+1
250  IF A = 22 OR A = 85 THEN 400
260  IF A = 43 OR A = 127 THEN 410
270  IF A = 64 OR A = 106 THEN 420
280  IF A = 129 THEN 500
290  GOTO 210
400  POKE 32,13 :VTAB 1:GOTO 210
410  POKE 32,26 :VTAB 1:GOTO 210
420  CALL -676: POKE 32,0: HOME:
     GOTO 210
500  IF D = 2 THEN GOTO 800
510  VTAB 6: PRINT " FOR HEX":
     PRINT "TOKENS, HIT": PRINT
     "RETURN ": CALL -676: D = 2:
     POKE 32,0 : GOTO 200
520  X$ = " ": H$ =
     "01234656789ABCDEF"
540  X% = ((B / 256) - INT (B /
     256)) * 16: GOSUB 600
550  X% = ((B / 16) - INT (B/16))
     * 16: GOSUB 600
560  PRINT X$: RETURN
600  XS$ = X$ + MID$ (H$,X%+1,1):
     RETURN
700  PRINT B: RETURN
800  VTAB 22:POKE 32,0:POKE C,186
810  END
```

APPLE SOFTWARE BANK

Apple Computer has now gotten their software bank under way. All Seattle area dealers have now received copies of Volumes 1 and 2 of User Contributed Programs in diskette form, and it works like this: buy a diskette or tape (or bring your own) to your dealer, and ask to see his catalog of User Contributed Programs, then select those you want and copy them to disk or tape. Depending on dealer policy, these programs will be available at little or no cost. Apple Computer expects a new release about every two months.

MYSTERY PROGRAM CONTEST

The object of this contest is to write an **Integer Basic** program that does nothing whatsoever, and will be used as a contest in the December Call -Apple. First prize will be a Wozpak and $10 cash, or $25 cash if you have ordered the Woz pak. Second prize will be a Wozpak or $15 cash, and third prize will be a copy of the newest version of Programmer's Workshop. Ties will be decided on the basis of earliest postmark. Seattle entrants will have a three day postmark handicap and Washington and Oregon state entrants will have two day handicap. All entries must be received no later than November 21, 1978. Just follow these simple rules:

1. The program must be written in Integer Basic.
2. It must run on a machine with only 16K of RAM.
3. It must not require use of disk or printer. They may be optional, however.
4. The program must serve no useful purpose whatsoever.
5. End results must be identifiable (i.e., something must occur during the run of the program).
6. Algorhythms must be as devious as possible.
7. One or more Basic lines must change during run.
8. Author's name, address and phone must be in REM lines.
9. Bruce Tognazinni is disqualified!

WIG-WIZ CONTEST

Here is a simple contest to test your understanding of the Apple. Five prizes of Programmer's Workshop will be awarded for the five best answers. The same postmark handicaps will be observed as in the other contest. All entries must be received no later than October 20th. To qualify, each of the following questions must be answered:

1. What is the function of Line 0?
2. What is the function of the Pokes in lines 20-30-40?
3. What happens to the display while the program is running?
4. Describe how this program could be utilized as a subroutine in another program.

All you need to do is enter the program as shown in the listing below, and run it.

```
   0 POKE (( PEEK (202)+ PEEK (203
     )*256 )+37),17
   1 PRINT 3072
  10 REM  "WIG WIZ" BY RANDY WIGGINGT
     ON

  12 DIM C$(40)
  20 POKE 768,173: POKE 769,0: POKE
     770,192: POKE 771,41: POKE
     772,127: POKE 773,32: POKE
     774,168: POKE 775,252
  30 POKE 776,173: POKE 777,85: POKE
     778,192: POKE 779,173: POKE
     780,0: POKE 781,192: POKE 782
     ,41: POKE 783,127: POKE 784
     ,32: POKE 785,168
  40 POKE 786,252: POKE 787,173:
     POKE 788,84: POKE 789,192:
     POKE 790,76: POKE 791,0: POKE
     792,3
 100 GOSUB 490
 105 GOSUB 2000
 110 C$="800<400.7FFM E88AG"
 120 FOR I=1 TO LEN(C$)
 130 POKE 511+I, ASC(C$(I))
 140 NEXT I
 145 POKE 72,0
 150 CALL -144
 200 GOSUB 490
 210 GOSUB 2000
 300 CALL 768
 490 REM  GR LINES
 495 GR
 500 FOR I=0 TO 39: COLOR= RND (
     16): HLIN 0,39 AT I: COLOR=
     RND (16): VLIN 0,39 AT I
 510 COLOR= RND (16): VLIN 0,39 AT
     39-I: COLOR= RND (16): HLIN
     0,39 AT 39-I: NEXT I: RETURN

2000 CALL -936: PRINT "HIT ANY KEY TO
     CHANGE FLIP FREQUENCY"
2010 PRINT "TRY CONTROL AND EDIT KEYS
     , BUT NOT RESET": RETURN
```

& NOW, the AMPERSAND

Inside the elaborate labyrinths of Applesoft II there lurks a mysterious and shady character. This character can perform marvelous and incredible feats however, when beckoned forth to perform his many functions. This character goes by the name of Mr. Ampersand. We'll call him & for short. By cleverly using Mr. &, the user can extend Applesoft II indefinitely.   HOW ? ? ?

When Applesoft is executing a program, if it encounters a & at the beginning of a statement, a JSR to location $3F5 is executed. At this time, the user is free to do anything from assembly language. To fully utilize the capabilities of the ampersand, a list of some useful subroutines contained in the ROM version of Applesoft will be published in the October issue of Call -Apple.

& NOW, THE FURTHER ADVENTURES OF THE MYSTERIOUS AMPERSAND

(Continued from last month)

When last we saw this shady character named Ampersand, he was hiding in a memory location known only as 3F5. Now, as our story resumes, we find some of the Applesoft subroutines that Mr. & can use in the ROM version.

CHRGET (S00B1) - This routine gets the next sequential character or token from the program. At all times, TXTPTR (S00B8, SB9) points at the next character. After executing the & and jumping to location $3F5, Applesoft will leave TXTPTR pointing at the character immediately following the &, and leave that character in the accumulator register. Upon a JSR to CHRGET, the character next in the program is returned in the A-register, and the status flags are set as follows:

Zero flag - set if the character is a terminator (end-of-line or a colon ":").
Carry - Set if the character is non-numeric, i.e. not a digit. Cleared if the character is a digit.

CHRGOT (S00B7) - This subroutine gets the current character from the program. Whereas CHRGET increments TXTPTR to get the next character, CHRGOT does not change TXTPTR.

FRMNUM (SDD67) - This subroutine evaluates a formula expression into the floating point accumulator.

GETADR (SE752) - Subroutine converts the floating point accumulator into a two-byte integer, in locations $50 and $51.

GETBYT (SE6F8) - Evaluates a formula and converts it to a one-byte value in the X-register.

SNERR (SDEC9) - Prints "SYNTAX ERROR" and halts the program.

Note that after the user subroutine RTS's to Applesoft, the TXTPTR must point at a terminator, indicating the end of this statement. See example program on other page.

APPLE PATCHES

The May contact has listed the required patches to repair bugs in Applesoft I.

ARRAY INDEXING PROBLEM FIX

POKE 6331,32: POKE 6332,150: POKE 6333, 41: POKE 6334,234: POKE 10646,133: POKE 10647,177: POKE 10648,162: POKE 10649,5: POKE 10650,165: POKE 10651,132: POKE 10652,96

LONG LINE FIX

POKE 3050,234: POKE 3054,136: POKE 3055, 145: POKE 3056,158: POKE 3057,208: POKE 3052,251

"END" STATEMENT FIX

POKE 2048,210

FRE(0) FUNCTION FIX

POKE 6143,5

APPLESAUCE

The following recipe will save you loading time on your Applesoft programs. 1. Load Applesoft. 2. Do not "run" it. 3. Using the DEL command, delete lines 0, 940, inclusive. 4. Enter this line: 950 POKE 18, 255 This will give you a preset version of Option 1, Applesoft graphics mode. 5. "Save this at the beginning of a blank cassette and follow it with saves of programs written in Option 1. For Option 2, do the same except make line 950 read: 950 POKE 18, 0   Save this on another cassette and follow with programs in Option 2. Note: All Applesoft programs may be written in Option 1 if desired. The LET command is not required, and may be omitted. A REMark line may be handled like this: 530 GOTO 540:REM 540 SETS VARIABLE N. Applesoft will ignore all after the goto.

To set HIMEM at locations above 32767, use minus figures, i.e., HIMEM: (-32767-1) would set it at 32768; -32765 sets 32770.

THE POOR MAN'S HEX --
    DECIMAL -- HEX --
        CONVERTER

HEX	"DECIMAL		VALUE"		
	MSB	3rd	2nd	LSB	HEX
1	4096	256	16	1	1
2	8192	512	32	2	2
3	16298	768	48	3	3
4	16384	1024	64	4	4
5	20480	1280	80	5	5
6	24576	1536	96	6	6
7	28672	1792	112	7	7
8	32768	2048	128	8	8
9	36864	2304	144	9	9
A	40960	2560	160	10	A
B	45056	2816	176	11	B
C	49152	3072	192	12	C
D	53248	3328	208	13	D
E	57344	3584	224	14	E
F	61440	3840	240	15	F

A pencil, scratchpad and you - that's
all you need to convert HEX TO DECIMAL,
or DECIMAL TO HEX. Based on the fact
that unit, ten, hundred, and thousand
columns have a unique set of values
for hexadecimal, the above table will
assist you convert either way.

EXAMPLE: HEX TO DECIMAL
013C =?

MSB	3rd	2nd	LSB		DECIMAL VALUE
0	-	-	-	-	00000
	1	-	-	-	256
		3	-	-	48
			C	-	12
		total	-	-	316

EXAMPLE: DECIMAL TO HEX

14632 = ?
In the table, in the MSB column, the
number is less than HEX(4) and more
than HEX(3), so the MSB =3. To get
the third, put down   14632
(value for MSB(3))   -12288
                         2344

In the 3rd column, this is more than
HEX(9) and less than HEX(A), so the
3rd = 9. Again enter 2344
value for3rd(9)   -2304
                         40

in the 2nd column this remainder is more
than HEX(2) and less than HEX(3), so the
2nd=2. Again enter   40
value for 2nd(2)   -32
                            8

This remainder = 8 in the LSB column,
and = HEX(8). So, the HEX number for
14632 is 3928.

This might seem cumbersome, but it is
surprising how rapid this conversion can
become with a little practice.

        J.A. Backman

"POKE" THIS IN YOUR APPLE!
   by Bob Huelsdonk and Val Golding

A subroutine to find the Basic POKE statements for a machine language program or subroutine. Find the starting address of the routine you wish to Poke and convert that to Decimal. Now, in Basic, enter the following
program. (n=starting address)

```
1000   A=n B=A+19
1010   FOR I= A TO B:  PRINT I, PEEK(I):
       NEXT I
1020   X=PEEK (-16384):  POKE -16368,0:
       IF X 127 THEN 1030:  GOTO 1020
1030   A=A+20:  B=A+19:  GOTO 1010
```

This will give you 20 Poke statements at
a time, and Apple will wait for you to "Hit
any key" for a new page. Simple?

To find the starting address for a program
in Integer Basic, enter the command:
PRINT PEEK(202) + PEEK(203) * 256.

APPLE PATCH

Here is a patch to correct one of the few
bugs found in Applesoft II. The HTAB function will space 2 places further to the right than intended unless corrected with this
patch: POKE (HM-28), 202 where HM = the
value of HIMEM: for your Apple. This should be done after loading & prior to running.

LIST OF HANDY "CALL'S"

DECIMAL	HEX	FUNCTION
-1321	FAD7	Displays Registers
-676	FD5C	BELL,HALT,WAIT for CR
-673	FD5F	HALT, WAIT for CR
-868	FC96	Clear Cursor to Line End
-922	FC66	Line feed without CR
-912	FC70	Scroll up one line
-936	FC58	HOME, Clear screen
-958	FC42	Clear cursor to end of page
-1390	FA92	BRK, Display Address, Registers, Monitor
-336	FEB0	Scratch BASIC Program
-307	FECD	WRITE to Tape
-259	FEFD	READ from Tape
-155	FF65	Enter Monitor without RESET
-1052	FBE4	Immediate BELL
-211	FF2D	BELL, Print "ERR"
-468	FE2C	Move memory, must POKE: 60,61 LO Address / 62,63 HI Address / 66,67 Start LO new Address

Load any machine language subroutine address into $3F8, $3F9 (Decimal 1016,1017) and a CONT "Y" will jump to it.

ROUTINE TO FIND PAGE LENGTH

This handy little subroutine can be used in two manners; to fill a screen page with repetitive material or to determine the length of a screen page of print statements. Assume line 100 is a print statement with which you wish to fill the page.

```
100   PRINT " ":GOSUB 400
400   IF PEEK(37) < 18 THEN RETURN
410   POP:PRINT "FOR NEW PAGE HIT
      ANY KEY":CALL -756:GOTO 000
```

Line 400 reads the cursor and finds where it is on the page. If less than 18 lines, print more lines. Line 410 "Pops" the return address from the stack. Instead of Call -756 you could use INPUT A$ or Call -676, all of which are a means of halting the program to await further instructions.

SOME BASIC ENTRY POINTS

LIST	JSR $E04B	CALL -8117
RUN	JSR $EFEC	CALL -4116
RUN*	JSR $E836	CALL -6090
SAVE	JSR $F140	CALL -3776
LOAD	JSR $F0DF	CALL -3873

* = VARIABLES NOT DELETED

```
100 REM THIS ROUTINE ALLOWS EXECUTION OF M
ONITOR COMMANDS FROM > BASIC PROGRAM W
ITH RETURN TO BASIC

110 REM BY S H LAM, PRINCETON, N.J.

120 DIM C$(40)
130 INPUT "MONITOR COMMAND=",C$
140 C$( LEN(C$)+1)=" E88AG"
150 FOR I=1 TO LEN(C$)
160 POKE 511+I, ASC(C$(I))
170 NEXT I
180 CALL -144
190 END
```

SPACE FOR NOTES

Color Graphics

COLORS OF THE APPLE RAINBOW

       COLOR GRAPHICS IN ASSEMBLY

       SCREEN MEMORY MAP

       HIRES GRAPHICS

       and MORE!

USE OF APPLE-II COLOR GRAPHICS IN ASSEMBLY LANGUAGE

The APPLE-II color graphics hardware will display a 40H by 48V grid, each position of which may be any one of 16 colors. The actual screen data is stored in 1K bytes of system memory, normally locations $400 to $7FF. (A dual page mode allows the user to alternatively display locations $800 to $BFF). Color displays are generated by executing programs which modify the "screen memory." For example, storing zeroes throughout locations $400 to $7FF will yield an all-black display while storing $33 bytes throughout will yield an all-violet display. A number of subroutines are provided in ROM to facilitate useful operations.

The x-coordinates range from 0 (leftmost) to 39 (rightmost) and the y-coordinates from 0 (topmost) to 47 (bottommost). If the user is in the mixed graphics/text mode with 4 lines of text at the bottom of the screen, then the greatest allowable y-coordinate is 39.

The screen memory is arranged such that each displayed horizontal line occupies 40 consecutive locations. Additionally, even/odd line pairs share the same byte groups. For example, both lines 0 and 1 will have their leftmost point stored in the same byte, at location $400; and their rightmost point stored in the byte at location $427. The least significant 4 bits correspond to the even line and the most significant 4 bits to the odd line. The relationship between y-coordinates and memory addresses is illustrated on the following page.

The APPLE-II color graphics subroutines provided in ROM use a few page zero locations for variables and workspace. You should avoid using these locations for your own program variables. It is a good rule not to use page zero locations $20 to $4F for any programs since they are used by the monitor and you may wish to use the monitor (for example, to debug a program) without clobbering your own variables. If you write a program in assembly language that you wish to call from BASIC with a CALL command, then avoid using page zero locations $20 to $FF for your variables.

Color Graphics
Page Zero Variable Allocation

GBASL	$26
GBASH	$27
H2	$2C
V2	$2D
MASK	$2E
COLOR	$30

GBASL and GBASH are used by the color graphics subroutines as a pointer to the first (leftmost) byte of the current plot line. The (GBASL), Y addressing mode of the 6502 is used to access any byte of that line. COLOR is a mask byte specifying the color for even lines in the 4 least significant bits (0 to 15) and for odd lines in the 4 most significant bits.

These will generally be the same, and always so if the user sets the COLOR bye via the SETCOLOR subroutine provided. Of the above variables only H2, V2, and MASK can be clobbered by the monitor.

Writing a color graphics program in 6502 assembly language generally involves the following procedures. You should be familiar with subroutine usage on the 6502.

1. Set the video mode and scrolling window (refer to the section on APPLE-II text features)
2. Clear the screen with a call to the CLRSCR (48-line clear) subroutines. If you are using the mixed text/graphics feature then call CLRTOP.
3. Set the color using the SETCOLR subroutine.
4. Call the PLOT, HLINE, and VLINE subroutines to plot points and draw lines. The color setting is not affected by these subroutines.
5. Advanced programmers may wish to study the provided subroutines and addressing schemes. When you supply x- and y-coordinate data to these subroutines they generate BASE address, horizontal index, and even/odd mask information. You can write more efficient programs if you supply this information directly.

PLOT1 subroutine (address $F80E)

Purpose: To plot squares in standard resolution mode with no Y-coordinate change from last call to PLOT. Faster than PLOT.
   Uses most recently specified COLOR (see SETCOL)

Entry: X-coordinate in Y-Reg (0 to 39)

Exit: A-Reg clobbered. Y-Reg and carry unchanged.

Example: (Plotting two squares - one at (3, 7) and one at (9, 7))

```
LDY #$3          X-coordinate
LDA #$7          Y-coordinate
JSR PLOT         Plot (3, 7)
LDY #$9          New X-coordinate
JSR PLOT1        Call PLOT1 for fast plot.
```

SPACE FOR NOTES

HLINE subroutine (address $F819)

Purpose: To draw horizontal lines in standard resolution mode. Most recently specified COLOR (see SETCOL) is used.

Entry: The Y-coordinate (0 to 47) is in the A-Reg. The leftmost X-coordinate (0 to 39) is in the Y-Reg and the rightmost X-coordinate (0 to 39) is in the variable H2 (location $2C). The rightmost x-coordinate may never be smaller than the leftmost.

Calls: PLOT, PLOT1

Exit: The Y-Reg will contain the rightmost X-coordinate (same as H2 which is unchanged). The A-Reg is clobbered. The carry is set.

Example: Drawing a horizontal line from 3 (left X-coord) to $1A (right X-coord) at 9 (Y-coord)

```
LDY # $3               Left

LDA # 0$1A             Right

STA H2                 Save it

LDA # $9               Y-coordinate

JSR HLINE              Plot line
```

SETCOL subroutine (address $FS64)

Purpose: To specify one of 16 colors for standard resolution plotting.

Entry: The least significant 4 A-REG bits contained a color code (0 to $F). The 4 most significant bits are ignored.

Exit: The variable COLOR (location $30) and the A-Reg will both contain the selected color in both half bytes, for example color 3 will result in $33. The carry is cleared.

Example: (Select color 6)
```
LDA # $6
JSR SETCOL ($F864)
```

Note: When sitting the color to a constant the following sequence is preferable.
```
LDA # $66
STA COLOR ($30)
```

PLOT subroutine (address $F800)

Purpose: To plot a square in standard resolution mode using the most recently specified color (see SETCOL). Plotting always occurs in the primary standard resolution page (memory locations $400 to $7FF).

Entry: The x-coordinate (0 to 39) is in the Y-Reg and the y-coordinate (0 to 47) is in the A-Reg.

Exit: The A-Reg is clobbered but the Y-Reg is not. The carry is cleared. A halfbyte mask ($F or $F0) is generated and saved in the variable location MASK (location $2E).

Calls: GRASCALC

Example: (Plot a square at coordinate ($A, $2C))
```
LDA # 2C               Y-coordinate

LDY # $A               X-coordinate

JSR PLOT (F800)
```

SCRN subroutine (address $F871)

Purpose: To sense the color (0 to $F) at a specified screen position.

Entry: The Y-coordinate is in the A-Reg and the X-coordinate is in the Y-Reg.

Exit: The A-Reg contains contents of screen memory at specified position. This will be a value from 0 to 15). The Y-Reg is unchanged and the "N" flag is cleared (for unconditional branches upon return).

Calls: GBASCALC

Example: To sense the color at position (5, 7)
```
LDY # $5               X-coordinate

LDA # $7               Y-coordinate

JSR SCRN               Color to A-Reg.
```

GBASCALC subroutine (address $F847)

Purpose: To calculate a base address within the primary standard resolution screen memory page corresponding to a specified Y-coordinate. Once this base address is formed in GBASL and GBASH (locations $26 and $27) the PLOT routines can access the memory location corresponding to any screen position by means of (GBASL), Y addressing.

Entry: (Y-coordinate) / 2 (0 to $17) is in the A-Reg. Note that even/odd Y-coordinate pairs share the same base address)

Exit: The A-Reg is clobbered and the carry is cleared. GBASL and GBASH contain the address of the byte corresponding to the leftmost screen position of the specified Y-coord.

Example: To access the byte whose Y-coordinate is $1A and whose X-coordinate is 7.

```
LDA # $1A              Y-coordinate

LSR                    Divide by 2

JSR GBASCALC           Form base address

LDY # $7               X-coordinate

LDA (GBASL), Y         Access byte
```

Note: For an even/odd Y-coord pair, the even-coord data is contained in the least significant 4 bits of the accessed byte and the odd-coord data in the most significant 4.

USE OF COLOR MASK BYTE IN HIRES
by   Darrell Aldrich

This is a brief description of the use of the color mask byte (Location 812_{10}) for high resolution graphics in Apple Integer Basic.

This mask specifies an 8 bit pattern of plottable X coordinates, with the pattern repeating itself every eight coordinates, going from left to right. The bits in this byte represent the colors violet and green, alternately. (See Figure 1).

Suppose we want to mask off every other green bar on the screen as in Figure 2a, where "X" indicates a point we want masked off. Set up an 8 bit byte as in Figure 2b, with all masking bits=0 and all non-masking bits=1. Convert this value to decimal & Poke in decimal location 812.

		LSB							MSB	
Figure 1.		V	G	V	G	V	G	V	G	
		1	2	4	8	16	32	64	128	
Figure 2a.		V	X	V	G	V	X	V	G	
Figure 2b.		1	0	1	1	1	0	1	1	

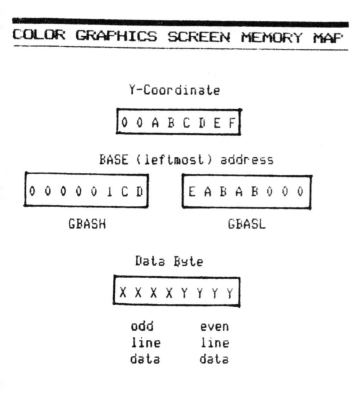

LINE		BASE ADDR		PG2 BASE ADR	
HEX	DEC	HEX	DEC	HEX	DEC
$0, 1	0, 1	$400	1024	$800	2048
$2, 3	2, 3	$480	1152	$880	2176
$4, 5	4, 5	$500	1280	$900	2304
$6, 7	6, 7	$580	1408	$980	2432
$8, 9	8, 9	$600	1536	$A00	2560
$A, B	10,11	$680	1664	$A80	2688
$C, D	12,13	$700	1792	$B00	2816
$E, F	14,15	$780	1920	$B80	2944
$10,11	16,17	$428	1064	$828	2088
$12,13	18,19	$4A8	1192	$8A8	2216
$14,15	20,21	$528	1320	$928	2344
$16,17	22,23	$5A8	1448	$9A8	2472
$18,19	24,25	$628	1576	$A28	2600
$1A,1B	26,27	$6A8	1704	$AA8	2728
$1C,1D	28,29	$728	1832	$B28	2856
$1E,1F	30,31	$7A8	1960	$BA8	2984
$20,21	32,33	$450	1104	$850	2128
$22,23	34,35	$4D0	1232	$8D0	2256
$24,25	36,37	$550	1360	$950	2384
$26,27	38,39	$5D0	1488	$9D0	2512
$28,29	40,41	$650	1616	$A50	2640
$2A,2B	42,43	$6D0	1744	$AD0	2768
$2C,2D	44,45	$750	1872	$B50	2896
$2E,2F	46,47	$7D0	2000	$BD0	3024

HIRES CAPABILITIES AND LIMITATIONS
by Darrell Aldrich

While written for Applesoft II, this article is also applicable to Integer Basic HI-RES graphics mode. The High Resolution Graphics screen is composed of 280 vertical bars (X coordinates), by 160 units high (Y coordinates). The even-numbered bars are violet in color, while the odd-numbered bars are green. The color white is produced by plotting adjacent green and violet bars. (Green+Violet=White.)

By plotting only on even bars, (even X coordinates), violet plots can be made. However, since we are plotting only 50% of the points on the screen, horizontal resolution decreases to 140 points. Plotting green is exactly the same as plotting violet, except plotting is done on the odd-numbered bars (odd X coordinates).

The HIRES routines produce the four available colors, (green, violet, white and black) by allowing us to mask off either the green or violet bars. Remember, when you set the HCOLOR variable (or location 812_{10}) for green, that a point may not be plotted on a violet bar, and the inverse is true for plotting violet on a green bar.

```
100 REM THIS ROUTINE DEMONSTRATES HOW THE
    VIDEO DISPLAY IS ORGANIZED

110 REM IT DISPLAYS HOW THE HIGH ORDER BIT
    S CONTROL "INVERSE", "NORMAL" AND "FLA
    SH" DISPLAYS

120 REM NOTE THAT THE VIDEO DISPLAY MEMORY
     LOCATIONS ARE NOT ARRANGED IN SIMPLE
    SERIAL FORM

130 REM THIS ROUTINE WILL POKE CHARACTERS
    INTO THE VIDEO DISPLAY AREA WITHOUT US
    ING TAB OR VTAB

140 REM THIS FUNCTION MUST BE USED IN ORDE
    R TO PEEK AT A LOCATION ON THE VIDEO S
    CREEN

150 REM "X" IS THE HORIZONTAL POSITION; "Y
    " IS THE VERTICAL POSITION WITH "0" AT
    THE TOP

160 REM  BY DAN CHAPMAN

170 CALL -936
180 FOR Y=0 TO 7: FOR X=0 TO 31:LTR=32
    *Y+X: GOSUB 220
190 POKE POS,LTR
200 NEXT X: NEXT Y
210 VTAB 12: END
220 POS=1024+X+128*Y-984*(Y/8): RETURN
```

SPACE FOR NOTES

Disk

DISK DISK DISK DISK DISK DISK

FUNDAMENTALS

FILE HANDLING

DOS PATCHES

IDENTIFYING BINARY PROGRAMS

DISK UTILITY PROGRAM

and MORE!

APPLE MASH   by Mike Thyng

Last issue I talked about the general specs of the PERSCI 277 eight inch floppy disk drive.   This issue I want to discuss some of the uses for a floppy disc and why anyone would even want one.

But first, let me digress. Since Apple has announced its own Disc II, why should I be telling you about the Persci floppy? Two reasons. 1) Computer Components announced its own floppy as available before Apple did, and 2) I'm using one in another system.

WHY would you want a floppy disc?

The two tasks that a floppy performs most often are program storage and data file storage. I feel that data file storage is the most important use you can put your floppy to. Files--data files--can be written in three basic ways. A file is a list of data grouped together for subsequent retrieval. There are three common ways of reading or writing data files. (You might think of this in terms of INPUT or PRINT).

1) SEQUENTIAL - This writes out your data in the same order it was read into the file.

2) RANDOM - This allows you to get your data any way (i.e., in any order) that you choose. Your records are accessed by their relative number on the file.

3) INDEXED SEQUENTIAL - This is by far the most flexible for a programmer, but is the most complex of the three accessing methods and costs (read wastes) a lot of side overhead. For your early needs, skip this one.

All files are composed of records. Records are made up of fields or variables. A typical kind of file is a Name & Address file.   In this, the file would be the names and addresses of, say, all the Call -Apple club members.   (Mike, you may have hit upon something! ...ed.) The record would be all the information about one club member. It might contain seven fields (or variables). For example:

APPLE MASH

1)   Name
2)   Street Address
3)   City
4)   State
5)   Zip Code
6)   Telephone number
7)   Special interests

The Persci 277 would be able to read 2000 records in five minutes. If you wanted to read and print all the names of the people in your name and address file, your printer is liable to be slowing you down, not your floppy disc system.

APPLE MASH   by   Mike Thyng

ARRAYS

This issue we'll discuss numerical arrays and dimensioning of single variables. We'll find out what an array is, how to use one and why it is so useful. Next issue, we'll discuss alpha variables and touch on matrices - arrays of multiple dimension.

First, what is an array? An array is a collection of related variables. You can tell one variable from another by using a subscript. A subscript is an independent variable that you use to access (there's that word from our disk file series) data from the array. As the subscript changes, so does the variable you will be getting data from. Note well- the data does not change when you change the value of the subscript; only the variable changes.

An example of a numerical array would be $A(1), A(2), ..., A(n)$, where the variable is A and the subscript is n. You might want a collection of numerical variables - an array - to store the passing distance of Seahawk quarterback Jim Zorn. So in our example, $A(1)$ would be the value in yards that he threw in pass one; $A(2)$ the distance in pass two and so on for as many passes as we want to record. Which brings me to an important point in our collective understanding.

Before we start our array, we must decide how many elements - in our example, passes - we plan to record. Let's choose 95. Now we need to tell the computer that we want to set aside space to record the distance for 95 passes. We do this with a DIM (or dimension) statement. DIM A(94) sets aside space for exactly 95 variables, $A(0)$ through $A(94)$. This is the most efficient use of the array space. In actual practice though, most programmers would just DIM A(95), then they could just refer to the last array element as $A(95)$. The element known as $A(0)$ would then become an extra variable that could be used for another purpose. You could also use DIM A(y) to set aside array space. However, you must then set y equal to 94 or 95, prior to the dimension statement, else your only element will be $A(0)$.

O.K. Now we've decided what our array A represents, we have set aside space for it. Now we need to set some data into it. We could set each of the 95 variables equal to the values we want to record.

```
A(1) = 23
A(2) = 50
    :
    :
A(95) = 46
```

But that's not really putting the computer to its best use. A better way would be:

```
100 INPUT "NEXT PASS "; A(N)
110 N=N+1
120 IF N < 96 THEN 100
200 REM  OTHER LOGIC FOLLOWS
```

An array is really useful (in 25 words or less) because you can access a bunch (technical word) of variables without writing separate logic statements for each one. As an example, if we assigned names to each of the 95 variables we used to record Jim Zorn's yardage, we'd have to write statements naming each of them individually. With the array, all we'd have to do to say, average them all, would be the following:

```
FOR N= 1 to 95
TOT = TOT + A(N)
NEXT N
AVER= TOT /95
```

ask your boss for arrays!

APPLEMASH

By Mike Thyng

Last time, we talked about single dimensioned numerical arrays. We also considered how and why the DIMension statement works. This time, we'll look at Alpha String arrays, INTEGER and Floating Point arrays and Multi-Dimensioning.

First some basics. We must tell the computer what type of data we're working with. Let's consider a variable called A. If we want A to store numeric values with results from "hard core" mathematics, we're talking about floating point variables, conveniently thought of as numbers with decimal points 5.6, - 8.13, .00477, etc. If we need counters or simple arithmetic variables without decimals, then we'd use integers. Now, when we want alphabetic data, like names or alphanumeric data like addresses or secret formulas (formulae) then we need string variables. For our example of A, A would be floating point, A% would be integer and A$ would be string or alphanumeric.

Now back to arrays. Last time we talked about keeping track of Quarterback Jim Zorn's passing yardage with a numerical array. This time let's find a way to keep track of the whole team's 100 yard dash times. First we set up space for each team member. They're allowed 45 players, so we set up our players names by DIM PNAMES (45). PNAME is our variable (players name), $ denotes string, and 45 sets up space for 46 players. Remember: PNAMES (0) through PNAMES (45). We'll use 1 through 45. Next, DIMension for their times. PTIME (a floating point variable should be DIMensioned.) DIM PTIME (45). Now let's take a look at one approach to recording the necessary data.

```
10 REM ALPHA-NUMERIC ARRAY TEST
20 DIM PNAMES (45)
30 DIM PTIME (45)
40 SB = 1
50 INPUT "PLAYER   "; SB;"   "; PNAMES (SB)
60 INPUT "PLAYER   "; SB; "'S   TIME   "; PTIME (SB)
70 SB = SB + 1
80 GO TO 50
```

This won't let you do much with the data you'd record, but after you've recorded players and times, you can refer to a player and his time with one subscript. That is PNAMES (18) and PTIME (18) refer to the player. This gives you an idea of how alpha and numeric arrays can work together.

Multi-Dimensional Arrays are set up like this:

DIM A (6, 5, 4). They're great for games and solving linear algebra through matrices. But that's outside the scope of this article. In example A (6, 5, 4) a down to earth use might be that you want to keep track of how many sales your salesmen are making in 4 attempts in each of 5 areas. Let's say you have 6 salespeople. Each one has a salesperson number. Each one must try to sell some gizmos in each of 5 areas. In each area the salesperson gets 4 chances. So, with multi-dimensioning you can record the number of sales per area per salesperson.

Again, as with single dimension arrays, you're setting aside space for your variables. For our 6 x 5 x 4 array above, we set aside places for 120 variables. I've had some arrays in testing that were 8 dimensional. I suppose core size is the only limitation on how many dimensions you can have, though it's really not practical to go much beyond 3 dimensions.

Next issue, we'll discuss how to use the APPLE Disk "T" files, random access — great stuff.

There is one bit of philosophy I want to end with. If it was more practical to have million byte core computers, then arrays of 8 or even more dimensions could be used instead of disk files. Remember, accessing data from an array is MUCH faster than accessing it from disk. In an array there is only solid state electronics between you and the data. On a disk file there's that mechanical arm and rotating diskette which must coordinate before you can get your data. Arrays are faster. Disks are more practical. I'll try to teach you how to use both. It is up to you to decide which is best for your application.

SPACE FOR NOTES

DISK II AND YOU
by John Covington

Finally!!! Disk II is out. If you're lucky, you will be able to play with one in your local computer store until yours arives from Cupertino. That is what I have been doing this last week, and this article comes from using the disk and my varied background in Data Processing. Hopefully, I'll be able to explain some of the HOWS and WHYS of the disk system and clear up some of the blind spots in Disk II's documentation. So let's get on with it and explore the mysteries of DOS.

DOS is simply short for DISK OPERATING SYSTEM, the heart of Disk II. With it, Apple is able to talk to the disk and treat it like any other I/O device. The DOS is just a program (which resides in the top of RAM) so like Applesoft, if you write over it, you can kill it. However, with normal use, you don't have to worry about that. If you are like me and have only 16K of RAM, the DOS will lock you out of using HIRES, because HIRES Page 1 uses your upper 8K of RAM. Now, let's bring the DOS up and find out how to use it.

HOW DO YOU DO THAT???
First, follow the instructions that came with the Disk System and plug the controller card into slot 6 in your Apple (with the power off). Then connect the ribbon cable from the drive into the controller card connector marked "Drive 1" (on the top of the card) and power your Apple up and hit reset twice. Insert the master diskette in the drive and type a 6 (for slot number), followed by Control P. This will bootstrap in the DOS and bring the disk system up. If all goes well you will see some titles and an Integer Basic prompt. This means DOS is up and you can begin running programs.

One of the first to run is the COPY program, but there is a hitch; it requires two drives. I'm sure the owner of your local computer store

One of the first to run is the COPY program, but there is a hitch; it requires two drives. I'm sure the owner of your local computer outlet will let you run this program in his store, using your drive as the second drive. The purpose of running the copy program is to duplicate your master. It may save both of you a lot of headaches later. (We found out the hard way. ...ed) The reason is your master can be lost in a number of ways, ranging from oxide breakdown to operator error. Therefore it is prudent to have a backup disk to recover from.

To copy your master, you must first initialize a blank disk. To do this, boot the DOS up and then enter a short Integer Basic program (as per example) and use the INIT routine as follows:
    INIT (program name), V(vol. no.), S(slot no.), D(drive no.). Then run the COPY routine and Disk II will make you a second master.

WHAT's THIS INIT THING???
The INIT command INITializes new disks. Because the Apple system uses soft sector drives, the floppies must be formatted to fit the DOS software. Any mini-floppy has 35 tracks (similar to a track on a phonograph record, except it does not spiral in; it meets itself after one revolution.) each of which must be divided into a certain number of sectors (a sector is where the data actually goes, and is composed of 256 bytes). To perform the INIT, you must have an Integer Basic program in RAM, which serves as a model for the formatter. It can be any runable Basic program, but keep it short, as this program will automatically run each time the disk is booted. The short program listed on Page 4 will serve as well as any, and will also call the catalog up for you each time you boot the disk up. Well, I guess I've given you enough to make you dangerous!

HAPPY DISKING!

APPLE MASH by Mike Thyng

BASIC FILE HANDLING

In the previous articles, we've discussed
types of files - sequential and random -
and general facts and figures about the
PERSCI floppy disk drive.
This issue I'd like to explore some of
the actual commands necessary to get
data to and from the diskettes.
Before you can write a file, you have
to do something called "opening" it.
This defines to your program that some
related data - let's say names and
addresses - is going to be available
for your use and can be referenced
by the name you give your file. If
you want to access (either read or
write) to your file you need to specify
OPEN AFILE. (AFILE is the name I gave
a file for example).
What if you want to write a whole new
file that hasn't existed in your system
before. Fine, use the FILE statement.
FILE BFILE opens a file called BFILE
and makes it available to you to write
sequential data.
FILE BFILE(130) opens a file called BFILE
that hasn't previously existed also. But
the difference is that each record you
write will be allowed to be a maximum
size of 130 bytes. You would use the
FILE BFILE(130) format whenever you
wanted to deal with random files.
Personally I use the random file format
exclusively. It gives me greater
flexibility for file handling. You
can always read a random file sequentially
but the reverse isn't true.
So now we've gotten into 2 files; AFILE
we'll use for gaining previously stored
information, and BFILE we'll use to write
new information.
To get the information from AFILE, you need
to READ # 1; field 1, field 2, field 3 ....
The READ is comparable to
The READ command is to a disk (or tape) file
what the INPUT command is to the keyboard.
The #1 is a direct reference to AFILE -
the first file opened. Fields 1, 2, and so
on are the variables you output to AFILE
when you wrote it.

To output data to BFILE we will do something
a bit more familiar. PRINT #2, 14; field 1,
field 2, field 3 .... The PRINT portion of
this command works the same as for output to
your CRT. The #2 means you are referencing
BFILE - which was the second file you opened.
14 refers to the fourteenth record on the
random file BFILE. Fields 1, 2, and 3 are
the same as for AFILE.
Later in your program close to the end you
must CLOSE files AFILE and BFILE. Why?
To keep the data. Writing to and reading
from disk files means you must get used to
a discipline known as file handling. Errors
in file handling can cost you a bundle in
effort to recover lost files. If you've
written data to a file but not closed the
file when you're through with it, you might
lose all the data that you stored. I can't
say always because sometimes the operating
system gives you a break. CLOSE 1, 2
will close AFILE and BFILE.
Not closing a file is like putting marbles
in a box without a bottom. When you try
to use it, your data isn't where you can
easily get to it.
Next time, some preliminary comments about
the APPLE II disk.

DOS PATCHES

Here are patches that will correct two of the bugs that occurred in earlier versions of DOS. Just follow the directions exactly as given below.

CORRECTION NO. 1

The MASTER.CREATE program does not always function correctly. Boot the Master diskette and type the following:

```
UNLOCK MASTER.CREATE
LOAD MASTER.CREATE
97 X=PEEK(1528)
100 PRINT "<CTRL><D>BLOAD RAWDOS"
105 POKE 14313,X:POKE 14327,X
110 CALL 6912:END
SAVE MASTER.CREATE
LOCK MASTER.CREATE
```

CORRECTION NO. 2

In Applesoft II, reading or writing data to a file will not work on a line number over 255. Boot the Master Diskette and type the following (do not type "hit reset"):

```
UNLOCK RAWDOS
BLOAD RAWDOS
(hit reset)
25D6: 4C D5 3F
25DC: 2E
3FD5: E8 F0 01 60 4C DD 25
3D0G
BSAVE RAWDOS,A$1B00,L$2500
LOCK RAWDOS
```

Next, initialize a diskette through the MASTER.CREATE program. Whenever this newly initialized diskette is booted, Applesoft II will work properly with READ and WRITE Statements. Also note that any slave diskettes initialized from the corrected master diskette will also have the problem corrected.

SAMPLE FILE HANDLER

Here is a short and sweet program by Bob Huelsdonk that demonstrates (and will establish) files for data handling, using the DOS.

```
8    REM    BOB HUELSDONK
9    REM    9/12/78
10   REM * SAMPLE FILE HANDLER *
11   D$ = "": REM  CTL D IN QUOTES
12   GOTO 20
13   REM   REMOVE LINE 12 AFTER RUN
     NING ONCE
14   PRINT D$;"NOMON I,O,C"
20   GOTO 500
30   REM ***  UNLOCK FILE  ***
32   PRINT D$;"UNLOCK";FI$
34   RETURN
40   REM ***  OPEN FILE  ***
42   PRINT D$;"OPEN";FI$;",L100"
44   RETURN
50   REM ***  READ FILE  ***
52   PRINT D$;"READ";FI$;",R";R1
54   INPUT A,A$,B$
56   PRINT D$
58   RETURN
70   REM ***  WRITE FILE  ***
72   PRINT D$;"WRITE";FI$;",R";R1
74   PRINT P: PRINT C$: PRINT E$
76   PRINT D$
78   RETURN
90   REM ***  CLOSE FILE  ***
92   PRINT D$;"CLOSE"
94   PRINT D$;"LOCK";FI$
96   RETURN
500  REM ***  INPUT DATA  ***
510  HOME : PRINT : PRINT "DATA I
     NPUT"
515  PRINT : INPUT "WHAT FILE NAM
     E? ";FI$
520  R1 = 0
530  INPUT "A NUMBER (-99 TO READ
      BACK)";P
535  IF P =  - 99 THEN 585
540  INPUT "A PHRASE";C$
550  INPUT "ANOTHER PHRASE";E$
560  GOSUB 40: REM  OPEN
570  GOSUB 70: REM  WRITE
580  R1 = R1 + 1: GOTO 530
585  GOSUB 70
590  GOSUB 90
600  REM ***  READ BACK  ***
610  HOME
620  PRINT : INPUT "DO YOU WISH T
     O READ THE FILE NOW? ";Q$
630  IF  LEFT$ (Q$,1) <  > "Y"
     THEN 1000
640  GOSUB 40
645  R1 = 0
650  GOSUB 50
655  IF A =  - 99 THEN 1000
660  PRINT A: PRINT A$: PRINT B$
670  R1 = R1 + 1: GOTO 650
1000  REM *** QUIT ***
1010  GOSUB 90
1015  PRINT D$;"MON I,O,C"
1020          END
```

PROGRAM TO INITIALIZE A DISKETTE

```
100 CALL -936:PRINT " (insert your name,
    address and phone)"
200 PRINT "THIS DISK CONTAINS INTE-
    GER BASIC PROGRAMS" (or game
    programs, etc.)
300 FOR I=1 TO 1000: NEXT I:  CALL
    -936
400 PRINT "DᶜCATALOG":END
```

Note: In line 400 after the first quote, hit the Control key and the "D" key at the same time. This is how the disk system responds to commands within a Basic program, with Control D in a print statement.

EDITORIAL by Val J. Golding

The big news story of this issue is obviously the arrival in town of Disk II and Applesoft II ROM. Rather than do a review, we have hidden behind the pretext of an editorial to state our feelings on the failings of Disk II and A/S ROM (I've got a feeling I'm failing? (Oh dear!))

Applesoft II ROM for $100 is like buying 10K of memory for less than half price, since it frees that amount of RAM for program use. Unfortunately, according to the documentation, the Applesoft ROM and disk versions are incompatable, although it is relatively easy to convert one to the other. However, in our estimation, the nusance factor is of prime importance, since one of the reasons for purchasing either version of Applesoft was to have it instantly accessable. One of the plans for our library was an Applesoft Pak. Now it appears we will have to make a Pak in three different versions, cassette, ROM and disk. (The documentation does not indicate whether the cassette version is compatable with either of the others.

The new Applesoft manual comes coverless, and commences with eight pages of corrections and additions to the manual.

This indicates a lack of planning by Apple Computer in rushing to get the ROM board into production without fully completing and checking the documentation. It is inexcusable for a computer system which is designed to plug in and run, and used by a pure beginner. Additionally, the HIRES color commands we found so helpful in the cassette version, DRAW, XDRAW, ROT=, SHLOAD and SCALE=, are not available in the ROM version. This means that even though one has the ROM card, one must also have the cassette version in order to use those commands.

The above shortcomings pale, however when one looks at the documentation accompanying the Disk II. While the information is all there, it is arranged in more or less haphazard manner, and concrete examples are missing. Jeff Raskin (who wrote the excellent manual on Integer Basic) where are you? No doubt the instructions can be easily understood by anyone. with computer background, but how about all us newcomers, Apple?

Finally, because DOS uses the COUT and KEYIN routines at $36 and $38, it is not possible while the DOS is up, to use the printer driver routine from the red manual. We have an Integral Data IP-225 printer, which works just fine at 1200 baud from the red book routine (modified), but it is not possible to run the printer without first killing the DOS. Of course, we could always get an Apple parallel printer card for $180, and that might solve the problem...

But before you change your mind about buying, let us remind you that all of the above is relatively minor and we believe both the disk and ROM are a wise investment. We would not be without either, having once had the opportunity to use them.

IDENTIFYING BINARY DISK PROGRAMS

Here are two ways to help you save and identify binary (machine language) programs on disk. First, follow this procedure, (which conflicts with the method suggested by Apple Computer), for BSAVEing your machine language programs: 1. If DOS is not up, boot it up. 2. CALL -151 (This puts you in Monitor without resetting. 3. load your machine language program from tape. 4. Control C back to Basic (or Applesoft). 5. Type "BSAVE PROGRAM,Aa,Ll" (where a= starting address and l= length). 6. Enter a NEW command (to insure nothing is in memory) and type "SAVE PROGRAM A$a L$l". What this accomplishes is to save a "dummy" Basic program (composed of nothing) which identifies where the binary program stores.

Another problem may occur where you have an existing binary program on disk and would like to copy it. This is a wee bit difficult if you have forgotten the address or length. To this end, we have written a program called "BINADR", which will load a binary program and tell you its address and length. It appears on this page.

Finally, a housekeeping hint, not directly related to the foregoing. We use this little trick to show when a disk is full. Again, this involves SAVEing a "dummy" program, and we do the title in inverse, to make it stand out.

POKE 50,63. PRINT "THIS DISK FULL". POKE 50,255. Now the words "THIS DISK FULL" will have appeared on the screen in inverse form and you should next type "SAVE". Then, using the escape (edit) keys, trace over the inverse characters and hit return. You now have a program named "THIS DISK FULL", and the title is displayed in inverse video!

```
50 REM   BINADR BY VAL J GOLDING

51 REM   APPLE PUGETSOUND PROGRAM
         LIBRARY EXCHANGE

52 REM   WRITTEN IN INTEGER BASIC
```

```
53 REM   THIS PROGRAM OUTPUTS A$ &
         L$ INFO FOR BINARY PROGRAMS

100 GOTO 500
110 IF PEEK (77)<64 THEN 150
120 PRINT 16384: REM SET LOMEM:16384

130 DIM FILE$(40): GOTO 160
140 PRINT 2048: END : REM RESET LOMEM

150 PRINT (( PEEK (77)-5)*256): GOTO
    130: REM LOMEM FOR 16K MACHINE

160 D$="": REM  CONTROL D
170 PRINT D$;"NOMON C,I,O"
180 TEXT : CALL -936: VTAB 14: INPUT
    "INPUT FILE NAME ",FILE$
190 IF FILE$="" THEN 180
200 PRINT D$;"BLOAD ";FILE$;",V0"

210 IF PEEK (77)>127 THEN 400: REM GO
    TO ROUTINE FOR 48K MACHINE

220 REM FIND POINTERS

230 HM= PEEK (76)+ PEEK (77)*256
    :LS=HM+5045:HS=HM+5046:START=
    PEEK (LS)+ PEEK (HS)*256
240 LL=HM+5027:HL=HM+5028:LENGTH=
    PEEK (LL)+ PEEK (HL)*256
250 CALL -936: VTAB 10: TAB 6: PRINT
    "DECIMAL STARTING ADDRESS IS: "
    ;START: PRINT : TAB 6: PRINT
    "DECIMAL LENGTH IS: ";LENGTH
260 PRINT : TAB 6: INPUT "MORE ?"
    ,Z$
270 IF Z$="Y" THEN 160: GOTO 140

400 START= PEEK (-22091)+ PEEK (
    -22090)*256:LENGTH= PEEK (-22109
    )+ PEEK (-22108)*256: GOTO 250

500 IF PEEK (203)>127 THEN 550
505 PP= PEEK (202)+ PEEK (203)*256
    : REM REPLACE PRINT WITH LOMEM:

510 IF PEEK (PP)=98 THEN POKE PP,
    17: IF PEEK (PP)=75 THEN 110
    :PP=PP+1: GOTO 510
550 PP=( PEEK (202)-256)+256*( PEEK
    (203)-255)
560 IF PEEK (PP)=98 THEN POKE PP,
    17: IF PEEK (PP)=75 THEN 110
    :PP=PP+1: GOTO 560
```

A DISK UTILITY PROGRAM
by Val J. Golding

Perhaps this may be the first disk program published for Apple's new Disk II. If so, a feather for our cap! The "SAVE" program, listed in column two will ask the user to input the file names of six disk programs, start recording on tape and hit return. SAVE will then consecutively load from disk and save to tape, in one operation, the six named programs. A neat way to make a tape for a friend from your disk collection.

Since this program uses the Basic SAVE command under program control, it is necessary to enter the SAVE commands as something else and then go into memory and change them to SAVEs. If you don't know how to do this, here is another routine that will do it for you. Just substitute the command TEXT where you see SAVE in the program and then add lines 1100 to 1250 as given below and RUN 1100. This will convert the TEXT commands to SAVE. After this has run, you can DELete 1100 to 1250, as they are no longer required. This routine can be modified to change any token or Ascii character in memory to another one, and of course, the program SAVE can be modified to save however many programs you would like in one operation by adding or taking away input statements and SAVE and LOAD statements. Remember in line 1000, Z$="D$". A Control D must be within the quotes for the DOS to recognize a Disk command.

```
1100 REM PRGM TO CHANGE TOKENS IN MEMORY
1150 REM EN=MEMORY RANGE TO BE SEARCHED
1200 LOCN= PEEK (202)+ PEEK (203)*256
     :EN=LOCN+735
1210 REM  PEEK AT VALUE OF ORIG TOKEN
1220 IF PEEK (LOCN)=75 THEN 1250:LOCN=
     LOCN+1: IF LOCN=EN THEN END : GOTO
     1220
1240 REM POKE VALUE OF NEW TOKEN
1250 PRINT "CONVERTING ";LOCN: POKE LOCN,
     5: GOTO 1220
```

```
>LIST
  10 REM   "SAVE" BY VAL GOLDING 7/23/78

  20 REM   THIS PROGRAM SAVES 6 NAMED DISK
          FILES TO TAPE IN ONE OPERATION

  50 GOTO 1000
  60 POKE 0, PEEK (76): POKE 1, PEEK
     (77)
  70 POKE 76, PEEK (202): POKE 77, PEEK
     (203)
  90 PRINT Z$;"LOAD ";A$
 100 SAVE
 180 PRINT Z$
 190 PRINT Z$;"LOAD ";B$
 200 SAVE
 280 PRINT Z$
 290 PRINT Z$;"LOAD ";C$
 300 SAVE
 380 PRINT Z$
 390 PRINT Z$;"LOAD ";D$
 400 SAVE
 480 PRINT Z$
 490 PRINT Z$;"LOAD ";E$
 500 SAVE
 580 PRINT Z$
 590 PRINT Z$;"LOAD ";F$
 600 SAVE
 649 REM   INSERT 6 CONTROL G WITHIN QUOTES

 650 CALL -936: VTAB 10: TAB 10: PRINT
     "FILES SAVED TO TAPE"
 700 POKE 202, PEEK (76): POKE 203, PEEK
     (77): POKE 76, PEEK (0): POKE 77
     , PEEK (1): END
 999 REM   INSERT CONTROL D WITHIN QUOTES
1000 DIM A$(36),B$(36),C$(36),D$(36),
     E$(36),F$(36):Z$=""
1010 TEXT : CALL -936: VTAB 4
1020 INPUT "   FILE NAME ? ",A$
1030 INPUT "   FILE NAME ? ",B$
1040 INPUT "   FILE NAME ? ",C$
1050 INPUT "   FILE NAME ? ",D$
1060 INPUT "   FILE NAME ? ",E$
1070 INPUT "   FILE NAME ? ",F$
1080 VTAB 20: PRINT "START RECORDING AND H
     IT RETURN TO SAVE   THE ABOVE LISTED F
     ILES TO TAPE": CALL -676
1090 GOTO 60
```

PLEASE PUT ALL CRITICISMS
OF THIS PUBLICATION IN
THE SPACE PROVIDED BELOW.

CHECKBOOK CHANGES FOR DISK
BY GENE JACKSON

```
1110  PRINT " 8.   SAVE DATA "; PRINT
      " 9.   CHECK FILE LENGTH": PRINT
      "10.   QUIT"
1112  DZ$=""; REM  CTL D
1114  PRINT DZ$;"NOMON C"
1200  CALL -936: PRINT "ARE YOU GOING
      TO ENTER DATA FROM": INPUT
      "THE KEYBOARD 'K', DISK 'D' OR T
      APE 'T' ?",C$
1210  IF C$="T" THEN 1300: IF C$=
      "D" THEN 2100: IF C$#"K" THEN
      RETURN
2100  INPUT "REPLACE CURRENT DATA OR A
      PPEND TO IT (R/A) ?",L$: REM  DI
      SK LOAD ROUTINE
2105  INPUT "FILE NAME TO LOAD ?"
      ,N$: IF L$="R" THEN 2130: IF
      L$#"A" THEN RETURN
2110  BCM=LM:LM=CM+0: GOSUB 2130:
      LM=BCM: RETURN
2130  PRINT DZ$;"BLOAD CB.HDR ";N$
      :B=LM+A: IF B>HM OR A<Z THEN
      GOSUB 20000:CM=B
2140  PRINT DZ$;"BLOAD CB.FILE ";
      N$;",A";LM: RETURN
2150  P=LM: GOSUB 2
2155  D(5)=R(0):P=CM-S-S+0: GOSUB
      2:D(6)=R(0)
2160  A=CM-LM: IF A<Z THEN RETURN
      : PRINT DZ$;"BSAVE CB.HDR "
      ;N$;",A2048,L102"
2165  PRINT DZ$;"BSAVE CB.FILE ";
      N$;",A";LM;",L";A
2170  PRINT DZ$;"LOCK CB.HDR ";N$
      : PRINT DZ$;"LOCK CB.FILE "
      ;N$: RETURN
2610  INPUT "OK, TYPE IT IN- (NO COMMA
      S PLEASE) -",N$
2620  INPUT "DO YOU WISH TO SAVE TO DI
      SK 'D' OR TAPE 'T' ?",C$: IF
      C$="D" THEN 2150: IF C$#"T"
      THEN RETURN
3205  PRINT DZ$;"MON C"
```

A number of master diskettes were inadvertantly sent
out blank by Apple. If your brand new disk wont boot, this
possibly could be the cause.

USING GAME-PADDLE BUTTONS
by Steve Paulson

In looking over a few of the programs currently in our game-paks I happened upon two programs which could be improved through the use of paddles. They are: "Klingon Capture" and "Pin Ball" (marbles).

During the operation of these programs, one must control part of the game by operating the game paddle and part by "hitting" a key on the keyboard. This seems a waste of human maneuvers. By a few simple changes and yes, additions, these programs can be made more interesting and easier to operate.

In the game of "Klingon Capture" we can change one line and add another changing the game from a strictly one-man game to the possibility of two players. Here are the changes:

Line #4340: change to: KEY = PEEK (-16287): IF KEY > 127 THEN 4400

Add line #4342: KEY = PEEK (-16286): IF KEY > 127 THEN 4400

Change #4400 to: REM

These changes and additions will cause the paddle-buttons to be used in place of the keyboard. In this program two people can now play together. Paddle 0 will control vertical and paddle 1 will control horizontal movement of the ship. Both paddles will now fire the torpedos.

In the instance of "Pin Ball," we have a nice relaxing game that both children and adults can play. I have two young children interested in the computer and sometimes I like to have them experience it with me. "Marbles" is just the thing.

By changing two lines and deleting one, the kids can play the game without touching the computer. Here are the changes:

Line #2740: change to: F = PEEK (-16287)

Line #2750: change to: IF F < 128 THEN 2680

Line #2760: delete this line.

These changes will cause the paddle-button to drop the marble instead of the keyboard.

In the case of "Klingon Capture" an extra line is added permitting two to play, and the program is easier to use.

In the case of the "Pin Ball", one may now sit back in the chair and watch the marbles fall. This is quite a change from having to constantly reach over and hit a key.

These changes add a little more ease to the games and a lot more character. They alter the technique, making the programs more "professional" in style and lend a higher quality to one's programming ability.

Pay a little bit more and get a printer that's brighter than your computer. The BrighterWriter.™

When a few dollars more buys you a first-class impact printer, why settle for a toy? The Brighter-Writer gives you quality to start with. And versatility that stays even if you outgrow your present personal computer.

Built smart like the big ones.

The BrighterWriter's a smart printer. There's a microcomputer inside. It outwits even the bigger, higher-priced printers. So you get versatility to do all kinds of printing. And power to grow on.

 Prints fat, skinny, tall, small.*

This printer can be as creative as your imagination. Stretch out your char-acters. Squeeze them close. Make them high. Low. Bold. Banner. You name it.

Plugs into your computer.

Most popular personal computers interface to the BrighterWriter. Simply and quickly. Hundreds of BrighterWriters are working in Apple, TRS-80, Heathkit, S-100 and many other personal computer systems right now.

Pictures and fancy symbols.*

The BrighterWriter draws out your creativity. You can print drawings, graphs, diagrams, bold symbols, or just about any graphic you can imagine.

Picture your page as thousands of dots. The BrighterWriter can fill in the dots, plot them contiguously, stack them, or scatter them. And its special set of graphic characters simplifies the process.

Prints any character a typewriter can. Faster . . .

The BrighterWriter can print plain and simple. With 7x7 dot matrix clarity. You get all the letters, numbers, and standard symbols of a regular

typewriter. At up to 80 cps throughput.

Ordinary paper.

Fancy or plain, the Brighter-Writer prints on ordinary paper. Better yet, it prints on many shapes of paper. Single sheets. Roll. Fanfold.

Want more copies? The BrighterWriter prints multiple copies without extra adjustments.

Four easy buttons.

Operating the BrighterWriter couldn't be simpler. Up-front controls are easy to get to. A power

button to turn it on. A test button to self-test your printer. A paper feed button to advance the sheets or forms. A line feed button to advance the paper a line at a time.

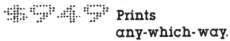 **Prints any-which-way.**

The BrighterWriter comes in two models. The IP-225, at $949, gives you a BrighterWriter with tractor-feed drive for precision forms control. This one can handle everything from labels to 8½" paper widths.

It has eight form lengths and gives you all the features of our IP-125.

A brighter buy.

Our IP-125, friction-feed, BrighterWriter has a 96 character set and prints on 8½" wide paper. Upper and lowercase. It prints expanded characters, too. You can choose a RS-232 serial or parallel interface. $799

Lots of goodies.

There's more. Choose all kinds of options for your BrighterWriter. Up to 132 characters per line, variable character densities, larger buffers, special graphics packages, interface cables, and more.

Give us a call or write. Integral Data Systems, 14 Tech Circle, Natick, MA 01760, (617) 237-7610.

Better yet, see the Brighter-Writer at the store nearest you.

 Integral Data Systems, Inc.

*Some of these advantages require extra-cost options

Printing

PRINT " PRINTER INFORMATION SECTION"

PRINTER DRIVER FIXES

IP 125/225 DRIVER

and MORE!

PRINTER DRIVER FIXES

by Bob Huelsdonk

Some protocol is a must if you use a printer with > 40 columns with your Apple. This comes about because it tries to write beyond the screen area and into the variables area in Integer Basic or into the operating system in Applesoft. The following will help prevent problems:

Start your printer driver routine with a JSR FC58. This will home the cursor and clear the screen. Do not return to the screen via FDFO. You will not get any output to the CRT but this is usually O.K. Unless you have the ROM version of Applesoft, there is also a problem using a PR#0. To solve this, use the routine given below to re-enter the CRT output with a call to 1008, if you load it at the address shown. This also resets the window width to 40 characters. For driver routines that are located in memory between $0300 and $03FF, there is also a conflict with the disk operating system, which will not permit you to directly call the printer. However, this can be overcome in most cases by addressing the printer under program control. In printing a program listing, a line must be added to the program as follows:

```
10 CALL 880 : LIST 100,900 : CALL 1008 : END

   03F0-    A9 F0      LDA    #$F0
   03F2-    85 36      STA    $36
   03F4-    A9 FD      LDA    #$FD
   03F6-    85 37      STA    $37
   03F8-    A9 28      LDA    #$28
   03FA-    85 21      STA    $21
   03FC-    60         RTS
```

Card Shuffling Caution

The last 90 days or so have seen a tremendous influx of peripheral equipment available for the Apple II, much in the form of plug in cards. Cliff Gazaway of Computerland has told us numerous sad tales of mishaps that have occured while changing cards. Here are two prime rules to follow:
1. **NEVER** plug a card in or out while the power is on.
2. Wait a minimum of 10 seconds after the power is off, before pulling a card.

HERE'S AN "OOPS FIXER" ©

J.A. BACKMAN   6-27-78

If you have dumped a program by hitting "RESET" when you meant to hit "RETURN" and C^C wouldn't bring the program back - - I'll bet the air was as blue around your APPLE II as it was around mine! - ! - !

A sweet little fix is a simple gadget that stops accidental keying "RESET" but does not stop its operation when it is needed. It does not hide the key, and doesn't require lifting a lid to get to it.

The gadget is made in a few minutes from an old - tired - empty cassette storage box lid. Just cut off 1-½" from the left end of the cover, shorten the remaining length to 2-¼", soften the plastic over gentle heat and bend the long flat side up about 15° 1-1/8" from the single edge.

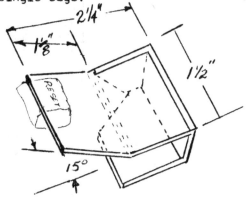

Now, to use this gadget, press down slightly on the lower right hand corner of the top cover of your APPLE II, just above the "RESET" key. This will make a thin gap - just wide enough to slip the narrowest side under the keyboard housing and the top cover. If the bend angle is right, the plastic shield will cover, and just clear the "RESET" key. There is enough tension from the top cover to hold it in place.

Wonder-of-wonders! ! ! the "RESET" key still works by pressing the cover, but, when you reach for the "RETURN" key - - your finger stubs. Voilà ! ! no more unintentional program dumps.

INTEGRAL DATA IP 125-225 DRIVER

If you own an Integral Data printer, you may be interested in these minor modifications to the Apple Red Manual teletype routine. The modifications are slight, changing only the window width and baud rate and adding a small delay loop to prevent printer buffer overflow, plus a turn off routine that restores window width to 40 columns. It loads from $0360 to $03E9 and is called from Basic with CALL 874, or from Monitor with $36BG. The Basic turn off call is 864. Window width is set at location $374, delay at $380 and baud rate at $3D4. It performs beautifully for us, running off a 20 mil current loop built on an Apple hobby board, taking data from the paddle output. Here's the disassembled listing

```
0360-   A9 F0         LDA    #$F0
0362-   85 36         STA    $36
0364-   A9 FD         LDA    #$FD
0366-   85 37         STA    $37
0368-   4C 39 FB      JMP    $FB39
036B-   A9 7D         LDA    #$7D
036D-   85 36         STA    $36
036F-   A9 03         LDA    #$03
0371-   85 37         STA    $37
0373-   A9 84         LDA    #$84
0375-   85 21         STA    $21
0377-   A5 24         LDA    $24
0379-   8D F8 07      STA    $07F8
037C-   60            RTS
037D-   48            PHA
037E-   48            PHA
037F-   A9 48         LDA    #$48
0381-   20 A8 FC      JSR    $FCA8
0384-   AD F8 07      LDA    $07F8
0387-   C5 24         CMP    $24
0389-   68            PLA
038A-   B0 03         BCS    $038F
038C-   48            PHA
038D-   A9 A0         LDA    #$A0
038F-   2C C0 03      BIT    $03C0
0392-   F0 03         BEQ    $0397
0394-   EE F8 07      INC    $07F8
0397-   20 C1 03      JSR    $03C1
039A-   68            PLA
039B-   48            PHA
039C-   90 E6         BCC    $0384
039E-   49 0D         EOR    #$0D
03A0-   0A            ASL
03A1-   D0 0D         BNE    $03B0
03A3-   8D F8 07      STA    $07F8
03A6-   A9 8A         LDA    #$8A
03A8-   20 C1 03      JSR    $03C1
03AB-   A9 58         LDA    #$58
```

```
03AD-   20 A8 FC      JSR    $FCA8
03B0-   AD F8 07      LDA    $07F8
03B3-   F0 08         BEQ    $03BD
03B5-   E5 21         SBC    $21
03B7-   E9 F7         SBC    #$F7
03B9-   90 04         BCC    $03BF
03BB-   69 1F         ADC    #$1F
03BD-   85 24         STA    $24
03BF-   68            PLA
03C0-   60            RTS
03C1-   8C 78 07      STY    $0778
03C4-   08            PHP
03C5-   A0 0B         LDY    #$0B
03C7-   18            CLC
03C8-   48            PHA
03C9-   B0 05         BCS    $03D0
03CB-   AD 59 C0      LDA    $C059
03CE-   90 03         BCC    $03D3
03D0-   AD 58 C0      LDA    $C058
03D3-   A9 14         LDA    #$14
03D5-   48            PHA
03D6-   A9 20         LDA    #$20
03D8-   4A            LSR
03D9-   90 FD         BCC    $03D8
03DB-   68            PLA
03DC-   E9 01         SBC    #$01
03DE-   D0 F5         BNE    $03D5
03E0-   68            PLA
03E1-   6A            ROR
03E2-   88            DEY
03E3-   D0 E3         BNE    $03C8
03E5-   AC 78 07      LDY    $0778
03E8-   28            PLP
03E9-   60            RTS
```

RETURN to TEXT from GRAPHICS

by Alan G. Hill

Here is a short routine that may come in handy if working on graphics programs when you need to frequently return to text mode to correct lines. Normally, you must hit control C, return, text and call -936 or escape @. This will permit you to hit reset, control Y and return. To load this routine, go to monitor and call the mini-assembler (F666G), and enter the following:

```
03F8:   JMP   $0300    ;Go to Control Y routine
0300:   JSR   $FC58    ;Clear scrn, home cursor
        PLA            ;Pop return adr off stack
        PLA
        JMP   $E003    ;Back to Basic
```

Miscellaneous

MISCELLANEOUS

A.P.P.L.E. LIBRARY

SAVE AN ARRAY

TIME SHARING

and MORE!

BYTES from the APPLE
Software Stuff, etc., etc., etc., etc., etc., etc., etc., etc., etc., etc., etc.,

by Val J. Golding

The BIG NEWS for this issue is APPLESOFT WORKSHOP is here! The cost is $6.41 postpaid, and orders will be accepted, subject to the following conditions: This preliminary version will be updated several times over the next few months. Updates will be available at $2.00 postpaid. This version is disk-dependent in that it requires disk for certain routines, including Append. Every attempt has been made to debug it, but some may still remain. Please allow 30 days for delivery on this and the other new Library Paks.

Library Paks 3 and 4 are expected to be available by the time you read this. Pak 3 will contain Home Ecpak 1, Musicpak 1 and more games. Pak 4 will contain a complete financial program, amortzation, etc., along with the usual compliment of games and demos. Price is $5.41 each, postpaid.

DOCUMENTATION PACKAGE

We have been able to obtain, through the kindness and courtesy of Randy Wigginton and Apple Computer, Inc., a superb package of Apple documentation, consisting of well over 200 pages. It is our intention to make this available to our membership for only slightly more than the cost of printing and shipping, for $12.50, postpaid. Because our print run will be limited to orders received, it will be essential for your orders to reach us no later than October 27th. This package will be distributed to local members at the meeting of November 21st, and they may deduct $2.50 from their remittance. Envelopes containing orders MUST be marked on the outside "WOZPAK" in order for us to handle them in the most expeditious manner.

The following is a partial list of contents:
Disassembler (12 pgs)
Cassette file handling (18 pgs)
Using Apple II color graphics (7 pgs)
Integer floating point package (23 pgs)
Sweet Sixteen (30 pgs)
Renumber-Append (27 pgs)
Use of read-write track sector (13 pgs)
Apple II Trek (14 pgs)
Lower case Apple (6 pgs)
Apple II system monitor (29 pgs)

USER GROUPS: you may obtain a copy for your group at no cost by submitting two original programs from your own group that may be distributed to our membership.

HOW OUR PROGRAM LIBRARY WORKS

In the last few weeks, we have been expanding very rapidly. So much so that the library has not really been able to fill requests on a completely current basis. We felt that it would be worthwhile to take some space, both to let all members know of recent additions to the library, and to acquaint new members with what is available. With the rapid changes, we have more or less been making policy on the go. A number of changes have been made in the manner in which we produce and distribute programs, with an eye to keeping both handling and reproduction costs to a minimum.

Currently, when we receive a request for an application blank, we also send out available software lists and prices. We have designed "Library Paks" to help new members establish their personal libraries. Each Library Pak has 20 or more programs in modular form, and cost $5.00 plus .41 postage (if from the club). The library Paks are available by mail from the club, or from participating dealers. Individual programs and/or modules may be copied at club meetings at no charge, or from dealers. This is also the way in which you will acquire new programs before they are assembled into Library Paks. Index lists of Paks may be obtained at meetings, dealers or with a S.A.S.E. Here's our current list:

Library Pak 1B	5.00
Library Pak 2 (ready about 8/1)	5.00
Programmer's Workshop II	5.00
Integer Basic Tutorial	15.00
Text Editor/Word Processor	45.00

We plan to distribute these to all area dealers. Some are in stock now. If you have ordered a Pak by mail and not received it, it will be along soon!
****
Any Ascii control character can be used within a print statement and will function under program control.
****

MODIFYING WORKSHOP

For those of you who may be so inclined and are inter ested in adding your own routines to, or otherwise modifying Programmer's Workshop, it is necessary to bring those high numbered lines down to where they are accessible. The Workshop's own renumber routine will help on this, but it is a operation. First run Workshop to set the poke statements into memory. Then reload Workshop and save lines 0 to 420 separately. Call them the "head", if you like. Then enter the following pokes, to set up the renumbering process:

```
POKE 2,32500 MOD 256
POKE 3,32500/ 256
POKE 4,2
POKE 5,0
POKE 6,32765 MOD 256
POKE 7,32765/ 256
POKE 8,255
POKE 9,255
```

Next call 776, which will accomplish the actual renumbering. When work is completed, Workshop can be renumbered back up using its own routine. Just use a starting number of 32765 and an increment of 1. Remember that the value of B in line 32765 is set to equal the exact number of bytes in the program. This can be verified by testing with the BYTES routine. The value of P in the same line may also need to be changed as it determines the GOTO used in the POKE routine. After restoring the original high line numbers, then use the Workshop's own APPEND routine to put the head back.

NEW PROGRAMS

The library is now assembling games and other applications into module form, 2 or three programs on a menu. So far, we have Gamepak 1 with Anne Apple, OneArm Bandit and an updated version of Zot!; No. 2 contains Hurkle, Multiply and Biorhythm, while "Programmers Workshop" is com — posed of Append, Examine Basic, Renumber, List by Page, Poke Routine Writer, and Pick a Base From ...   Blackjack , Checkers and Craps will be in the next Gamepak, while other new programs include Appleodian, Hamurabi and Life. Remember, we need your programs!

PROGRAM LIBRARY

DANNY'S TEXT EDITOR

This editor is designed to work with and print operating on the Apple parallel card. It is available in both a disk and cassette tape version. When ordering, specify disk or tape, also make and model of printer and slot number used by printer I/O card. This printer has a provision to output in lower case to the printer, and displays upper case as inverse video on the screen. It has most of the usual edit-functions, including line and character insertion and selectable line length. Requires 32K Ram memory. Cost $45.00

LIBRARY PAK 2

This Pak is now in production and comes with our Lcos: Limited Cassette Operating System. It contains 7 modules with 34 programs. Color Gamepak 1 (The ill-fated program 8 from Lpak 1B), Color Gamepaks II and III, Color Demopak II, Holiday Greetingpak, Battleship and Nightmare Gamepak. Cost $5.00. An extra .41 for postage would be appreciated.

PROGRAMMERS WORKSHOP (for Disk or Cassette)

Workshop is currently being produced in one version only, which includes additional commands for handling disk files. Therefore you need order one Workshop only. if you own an earlier version without disk commands, you can get an updated copy for just $2.00. Workshop is a utility module, designed to aid programmers working on their programs. it contains 16 routines with 11 commands on a menu. routines are: Renumber, Append from disk or tape, List by page, Poke Writer, Examine Basic, Bytes free and used, Kill, Save to disk or tape, Quit, Catalog, Number converter and Variable list. We recommend it also as a tool to learn more about how your Apple works. Cost $6.00.

APPLESOFT WORKSHOP

NEW PROGRAMS

We have been gratified by the number of new programs we have recently received, particularly from some of our out of state members. We would like to take this space to thank Danny Lambert, John Cook, Ed Avelar, Dave Gordon, John Backman, Mark Cross, David Garson, Doug Trusty and many others for their contributions. Many of these programs will be turning up in future Library Paks. And that is the name of the game. A.P.P.L.E. makes it possible for these programs to be enjoyed by all members. Program submission forms are available at each meeting, or by mail for sending a S.A.S.E. Let's keep the ball rolling and share your work with others.

ROUTINE to SAVE an ARRAY

Reprinted from Apple Stems, Vol I, No. 2, July, 1978, the newsletter of Apple Portland Program Library Exchange.

Here is a routine to save both integer or floating point real numbers in an Applesoft II array. This will not work in alpha strings until they are converted, using the CHR$ function. Any variable may be used.

```
90   TEXT : HOME : VTAB 5
100    PRINT "THIS PROGRAM DEMONSTRATES T
       HE USE OF ": PRINT : PRINT "STORE
       AND RECALL FUNCTIONS OF APPLESOFT
       II"
110    PRINT : PRINT : PRINT "FIRST WE WI
       LL GENERATE AN ARRAY 'A(10,3)'."
120    FOR X = 1 TO 10: FOR Y = 1 TO 3
140  A(X,Y) = X * Y: NEXT Y,X
160    PRINT : PRINT "HERE IS THE ARRAY":
       PRINT
170    FOR X = 1 TO 10: FOR Y = 1 TO 3: PRINT
       A(X,Y);: NEXT Y,X
210    PRINT : PRINT
220    PRINT "HIT ANY KEY TO CONTINUE": CALL
       - 756: HOME : VTAB 5
300    PRINT : PRINT "NEXT WE STORE THE A
       RRAY": PRINT : PRINT "START THE TA
       PE RECORDER IN RECORD MODE": PRINT
       : PRINT "AND HIT ANY KEY"
320  : PRINT : CALL  - 756
330    STORE A
340    HOME : VTAB 5: PRINT "NOW WE WILL
       ZERO THE ARRAY": PRINT : PRINT
370    FOR X = 1 TO 10: FOR Y = 1 TO 3:A(
       X,Y) = 0: NEXT Y,X
410    FOR X = 1 TO 10: FOR Y = 1 TO 3: PRINT
       A(X,Y);: NEXT Y,X
450    PRINT : PRINT "NOW WE WILL RECALL
       THE ARRAY": PRINT : PRINT "REWIND
       AND START RECORDER ON PLAY": PRINT
       : PRINT "AND HIT ANY KEY"
470    CALL  - 756: HOME : VTAB 5: PRINT
       "NOW WE WILL RECALL THE ARRAY": PRINT

490    RECALL A
500    FOR X = 1 TO 10: FOR Y = 1 TO 3: PRINT
       A(X,Y);: NEXT Y,X
540    PRINT : PRINT "AND NOW WE HAVE OUR
       ARRAY BACK": END
```

APPLE-SHARING

by Jeffrey K. Finn © 1978

Time-sharing is the way many large-memory, high-speed computers are utilized to maximize their production and return on investment. I'm sure you've already realized while using your Apple, that you're usually the reason it doesn't work faster. When you're sitting at the keyboard, you're not typing at the 120 characters per second that the Apple reads your cassette tapes. Nobody is blaming you. After all, you're only human. In the meantime, the disk is merrily reading in information at a rate in the average range of three or four thousand characters per second. But even the disk is not taking advantage of Apple's Central Processor Unit, the 6502, and its memory chips. They are screaming for characters which they are able to manipulate at a rate some fifty times faster than the disk. That is in the range of 200,000 characters per second. We're talking about memory chips with read access time in the hundreds of nanoseconds. (One nanosecond equals a billionth of a second.) This is approaching the speed of light which travels one foot in one nanosecond. Please remember that it physically takes a certain amount of time for an electrical impulse to travel through the length of the wiring itself.

You are probably as confused as I was when I first tried to comprehend the speed of Apple's Central Processor Unit, (CPU), and its memory. To put these figures in a more understandable ratio, let's slow the whole thing down like a slow motion movie. Suppose the CPU were to operate at a speed where it could manipulate a character somewhere in the range of 3/4 of a second. Relative to that speed, the disk provides one character every 1/2 minute. The tape cassettes are providing a character every 3/4 of an hour, and a good typist at a keyboard terminal can put in a character every three to five hours. Next, consider all the times you've stopped to think a second, just one second, about the next key to type. In the relative time frame we're using, a real second is like a whole day to your Apple's CPU. That CPU is in there asking itself, "Hasn't that fool at the keyboard sent me a character yet?"

As you can see, a CPU which uses a keyboard, or most any other mechanical input/output device for moving information, has a lot of free time in which it could be doing something else. A large central memory core is needed to keep the CPU working at its full capacity as well as handle the few large jobs which require large memory areas for data bases and/or intermediate results. In these large computer installations when large jobs weren't being run, it was found several small jobs could be run simultaneously by having the CPU processing a small job in one section of its memory while loading and unloading the other jobs in other parts of its core memory. The information is transferred to and from the core memory in complete blocks, usually via a hard disk system. Except in times of high demand, the fact that several jobs are being run is not perceptible to the individual user.

To keep the core memory filled with information for the CPU to process, a master program which does several things is run continually. (You might think of this master program as something similar to your Apple's monitor program.) This master program 1) Tells the CPU which of the programs in memory to work on next; 2) Keeps track of what the CPU is doing; 3) Keeps track of what sections of core memory are being used for what; 4) Keeps track of which input/output devices, (printers, keyboard terminals, card readers, tape decks, disk files), are ready to send or receive information; 5) Organizes input/output into logical and complete blocks of information; and, 6) Directs the movement of those blocks of information among the various input/output devices and the computer's memory.

Through this master management program, the CPU is kept continually operating at a speed close to its potential, and its associated core memory is kept as full as possible, thus maximizing the central computer's use. To further assist your understanding of this subject, the following is a description of a typical, but much simplified, operating sequence of one of these master, (time-sharing), programs. First the program checks all input devices to see if there are any that want to send information to the main computer. If it sees that a punch card needs to be read at a card reader, a signal is sent to the reader to "read." While the card reader is starting to feed the card through its reading mechanism, the program recognizes that someone has depressed a key at a keyboard terminal. It issues a command to store the code for the key depressed in a particular area of the hard disk. It then goes back to the card reader in time to get the code from the card being read and stores that in a different area on the hard disk. All this takes place in less than the blink of an eye.

The program continues this process until it gets a code from one of the input devices that says this is the end of the information (job) from this particular device. The program then checks the area(s) on the hard disk where it had been storing the particular input to see how much there is, and estimates how much CPU time the requested processing will take. If there is sufficient CPU time and available core memory locations, it will transfer the block of information from the hard disk to the core memory and tell the CPU in what order it should start work on the information beginning at that location in core memory.

At the same time, the time-sharing program is also checking to see what information the CPU has finished processing. When it spots some, it moves the block of completed work back out to the hard disk. It then searches for the specified output device to see if it is ready to receive the information. These output devices include printers, card punches, tape punches, monitors, etc. When the device is ready to receive the information, the time-sharing program sends the information to the device.

One of the input/output devices that can be used is a telephone port. It enables information coded in that computer's format and an agreed-upon code, commonly ASCII, to be transmitted and received by ordinary telephone lines. In order to transmit on telephone lines which carry only tones, a device called a Modulator/Demodulator (MODEM) is placed between the computer's telephone port and the telephone handset. (The sophisticated operations combine all this with automatic answering and dialing and connect to lines without a phone.) The MODEM changes the ASII coded information into tones and tones into ASCII code.

Obviously, for this system to work, there needs to be a MODEM at both ends of the telephone line — one at the end where the central computer is located, and one at the other end which must be connected to some kind of terminal. The terminal decodes the central computer's format, (seven or eight bits, parity, etc.), for transmitting characters and uses the decoded characters in the manner it has been built to present information. It could punch cards, print on paper, or be a TV monitor.

This is essentially the way time-sharing works, and through the use of the Apple Communication Card you can participate yourself using the card as the encoder and decoder for your Apple. It enables your Apple to act as though it were a "dumb" terminal which can only send or receive characters from the central computer. It also allows your Apple to be a "smart" terminal and process information received from the central computer utilizing some of the powerful graphic capabilities of Apple's software. The potential is boundless.

One thing that you should remember if you are getting a MODEM for your Apple, is that with the Communication Card, your Apple can act as either the central time-sharing computer or the terminal. This means that your MODEM should be able to operate in both "originate" and "answer" modes. These terms refer to an adopted convention where the terminal's MODEM, the one doing the calling, is known as the "originate" MODEM and the time-sharing system's MODEM is the "answer" unit. This is done so the two MODEMs can go through a "handshaking" procedure to align their timing and tone generators.

In this handshaking procedure, the MODEM you call sends out a tone which your MODEM hears. That tone is saying, "Hello! Hello! Anybody there?" Your MODEM sends back a different tone which says, "It's me! I think we're in tune!?" If everything is in order, the answering MODEM sends back tones which mean, "Yes, we're in tune and I'm ready to receive information." If you've followed the procedures for that particular time-sharing computer you should be able to read a message on your monitor that requests you to properly "log in" on that time-sharing system.

A more complete article on MODEMs, their operation, and how to build them, is contained in the May, 1978 (3-4) issue of the Northwest Computer Society's Northwest Computer News.

My article next month will be about methods to avoid the pitfalls I experienced while attempting to get the "log in" message to appear on my monitor. If you avoid these pitfalls, most any computer in the world that has a telephone port can be connected to your Apple. In this way your Apple can be enhanced to equal the capabilities of those computers.

There may be errors in my statements or calculations due to my own misunderstandings. Though some of the information I have presented would not pass the rigorous scrutiny of professional engineers or computer experts, I felt required to write an article for our Call -Apple from a layman's point of view. I did it as an encouragement to other A.P.P.L.E. members who have gained valuable information which should be shared. I would appreciate hearing from those who discover errors in my writing so I can correct my misunderstandings. Val can put you in contact with me.

The following program is a simple illustration of the time-sharing principles I have discussed. It is intended to demonstrate the speed with which the Apple can simultaneously accommodate incoming information from four sources and display it. Imagine the Apple's game paddles and swiches as four terminals and that they are connected to four Apple telephone ports. See what happens when you twist the dials or push the buttons. To illustrate the speed of the CPU, see what happens if you push both buttons simultaneously. How perceptible is the delay in the screen's display? If the display for both buttons' condition didn't change at the same time, you didn't push at the same time. Can you perceive the time difference needed to push the buttons so that the status of button 0 changes on one line of output and the status of button 1 changes on the next output line?

```
100 REM TIME-SHARING DEMONSTRATION

110 REM BY JEFFREY K. FINN 9/17/78

120 REM THIS PROGRAM DEMONSTRATES
    THE SPEED WITH WHICH THE CPU
    REACTS TO EXTERNAL, MECHANICAL
    INPUT. <INTEGER BASIC>

200 CALL -936
210 PRINT "PRESS ANY KEY TO STOP PRO
    GRAM": PRINT "PADDLE0 PADDLE1 SW
    ITCH0 SWITCH1"
220 POKE 34,2
230 A= PEEK (-16287):B= PEEK (-
    16286): IF PEEK (-16384)>127
    THEN 300
240 IF A>127 THEN 280
250 IF B>127 THEN 310
260 PRINT PDL (0), PDL (1),"OFF"
    ,"OFF"
270 GOTO 230
280 IF B>127 THEN 330
290 PRINT PDL (0), PDL (1),"ON "
    ,"OFF"
300 GOTO 230
310 PRINT PDL (0), PDL (1),"OFF"
    ,"ON"
320 GOTO 230
330 PRINT PDL (0), PDL (1),"ON "
    ,"ON"
340 GOTO 230
```

In this part of the article, I want to discuss the more standard format options for data transmitted by electronic means, how to modify the default settings on your Apple Communications Interface Card, and some of the time-sharing systems in the Seattle area which you may be able to access utilizing the interface card.

It was obvious to those in the electronic data processing field that carrying around boxes of punched cards or reels of magnetic tape was not an efficient method of transferring data from one electronic data processing device to another. Each manufacturer was devising his own hardware and formats to electronically transfer information. Luckily, however, the industry was able to get together on a standard format for transferring data by electronic means. This enabled devices from various manufacturers to communicate directly with one another. This standard is known as the serial RS 232 standard because the bits representing a character travel over a single line one after another. The RS 232 standard is used by virtually all the time-sharing computer systems which you will be able to access through your Apple II computer.

Within the RS 232 standard there are options available to accommodate special needs of various hardware manufacturers and software programs. One of these options allows data to be transmitted at various speeds. Typically, time-sharing systems use a 300 baud transmission rate. There are systems that run at the lower speed of 110 baud. Also, due to more reliable communication links and hardware improvements, some time-sharing systems operate at 1200 baud and even higher. Your AppleCommunications Board can be physically modified to operate at 1200 and 4800 baud.

The next series of RS 232 options are related to the format of the data bits being transmitted. There is a specified order of bits. Each of the bits has a specific function to perform. The first bit is known as the "start" bit and it gets everything ready to receive the 7 or 8 bits that represent a discreet character. After the "data" bits come down the wire one after another, there is a bit that can be used as a check to see if the data bits (usually the ASCII character code) were received properly. This check bit is known as the "parity" bit. If "even" parity was chosen, the parity bit should be received as "on" if an even number of data bits were transmitted in the "on" condition. If the receiving device counts an even number of "on" data bits and the parity bit was "on", it assumes it received the character correctly. If the count is not in agreement with the parity bit, the device activates its error routine. The parity bit can also be set to be "on" if the number of "on" data bits is odd. Finally, the end of the particular character transmission is signalled by either 1 or 2 "stop" bits.

Another option for tie-sharing systems not directly related to the RS 232 standard is the mode of transmission referred to as full or half duplex. Though not an absolutely correct definition, it can be stated that full duplex refers to a system in which the time-sharing computer sends the characters it thinks it received from the remote terminal back to the remote terminal. Only then does the remote terminal actually display the character for which a key has been pressed. Full duplex mode provides some ability to confirm that the characters being sent are correct because the host computer would return incorrect characters if the terminal's transmission had been garbled. With the increased reliability of the telephone lines, garbled transmissions are a less severe problem than they used to be. The half duplex mode simultaneously displays the character on the terminal's display and sends the character to the time-share computer. Most of the time-share systems that Apple owners will use will be of the half duplex type.

From this discussion I hope it is obvious that to utilize a time-sharing system, you need to know things in addition to your account number and password. Otherwise you will be frustrated by the fact that you can't get the computer to let you join the system. The characteristics that you must know about the particular time-sharing system you want to use include: (1) the speed at which the time-sharing system receives and transmits data (baud rate); (2) whether the data word is 7 or 8 bits in length; (3) whether there is an odd, even, or no parity check; (4) whether there are one or two stop bits; and (5) whether the system operates in the half or full duplex mode.

When I was getting started, I found some information in the original documentation for the communications card, (provided by Apple), which briefly indicated how the communications card accommodated these various characteristics. Basically, an appropriate value is entered into something called the ACIA register. This register is located on the communications board in the 6850 MOS LSI (Large Scale Integrated Circuit). I got hold of the Motorola Manual on the 6850 and determined how the value in this register affects the baud rate, the number of data word bits, parity and number of stop bits. The Apple documentation said the value was passed to the ACIA register through location S608E plus the slot number in which the communications card was located in the Apple computer. Since I'm not an experienced programmer, I devised the accompanying chart of decimal values for the ACIA register, and translated the hexidecimal location into the equivalent Apple Basic "poke" statement. I tried to poke the value I needed to run on the City of Seattle's Univac 90/80 computer into the ACIA register, but was not successful. Wendell Sanders of Apple, Inc., explained that in addition to the value being stored in the ACIA register, the value must also be entered into a RAM location in the Apple's memory. He graciously sent me an advance copy of additional documentation which Apple now includes with its communications cards.

Once you have poked the appropriate value for the time-sharing system you are using into the two locations, the value will stay there if you abide by these two rules. First, poke the value into the two locations immediately after you initiate the communications card with the command PR # 2, (use the number for the slot you use in your Apple for the communications card). The second rule is to avoid typing the "reset" key. The value will stay in the two locations even though you go back and forth between PR # 2, IN # 2, PR # 0, and IN # 0. I have noticed that some unusual things happen if the Disk Operating System is booted. I haven't been able to discern the pattern so my guarantee about the value staying put is voided if you are using the disk.

Editor's Note: The patches for checkbook in this issue to deactivate DOS may help in this instance.

I would like to emphasize the fact that the default values which are set automatically by the communications card will enable you to use the majority of time-sharing systems. If it weren't for the fact that my job involves using the UNIVAC 90/80, I probably wouldn't have bothered to research all this information.

Assuming the communications card is in your Apple II computer peripheral slot # 2, the following pokes are needed to set the ACIA register to work with time-sharing systems using data formats different than those provided by the default value:

POKE 2042, (Appropriate decimal value from table)
POKE -16240, (Same value poked into location 2042)

ACIA STATUS WORD VALUES

DATA WORD BITS		PARITY			STOP BITS		ACIA REGISTER VALUE (300 baud)	
7	8	even	odd	none	1	2	hex	decimal*
●		●				●	$Ø1	1
●			●			●	$Ø5	5
●		●			●		$Ø9	9
●			●		●		$ØD	13
	●			●		●	$11@	17@
	●			●	●		$15	21
	●	●			●		$19	25
	●		●		●		$1D	29

*Add 65 to find values for 11Ø baud
@Apple Communications Interface Card Default Values

Some of the time-sharing systems respond to the "return" key just as your Apple does. However, some need the ASCII code for "ETX" to accept information you are sending. While holding down the "control" key, type the character "C" for these systems. This causes your Apple to send the proper code for "ETX."

The word "modem" has come to mean Modulator/Demodulators which connect directly to phone lines. An "acoustical coupler" is a modem that has a cradle in which you insert the telephone handset's mouth and ear pieces. Most of us will probably get an acoustical coupler to use with our communications cards. Normally, these couplers have a switch for selecting the full or half duplex modes. Set the switch to full duplex. Then forget it. Control the duplex mode from the communications card via the Apple's keyboard.

There are several time-sharing systems in the Seattle area that are of unique value to Apple owners. One of the most obvious is the Dow-Jones investment package that the Apple Company itself is offering. One item I noted as particularly important is the fact you don't have to make expensive long distance calls to the east coast to get in touch with the Dow-Jones computer. All the major cities have a local number to call to join the system.

Another time-sharing system is available through the Northwest Computer Society, P.O. Box 4193, Seattle 98104. Their annual $7 dues gives you the opportunity to use the Nordata PDP-11 system for non-business purposes during non-business hours for only a 50¢ an hour connect charge. The system is self-documenting. This means that the instructions for using various pieces of the system can be called to your monitor by asking for "help." This system's primary programming language is a very extended BASIC. Also, it has about 150 games for the computer game freaks, (including several versions of Star Trek). The Society has recorded messages at 284-6160.

The University of Washington's Academic Computer Center (ACC) has a Control Data Corporation time-sharing system available for non-University activities if certain conditions are met. Commercial business uses are restricted to activities that can only be done on the ACC's computer because of a unique feature of the system. The rates charged are competitive with private commercial time-sharing systems. If you want to use the computer for educational purposes or are part of some kind of civic organization that has a need to use the ACC's services, the computer is available at a rate between the commercial and University-user rates. It is the responsibility of the non-University user to substantiate their need to use the ACC's computer. There is some effort involved in doing this, but it is worth it.

By far, this is the best time-sharing computer system from user's point of view. The resource center (library) in the ACC has plenty of handouts, reams of documentation and an ACC Newsletter to assist you in getting on the system. Also, there are video cassettes you can watch at your leisure in the resource center which explain the use of terminals and inter-active computer sessions. Consultants are provided at no additional cost to assist you if you are having trouble. The system has a high degree of self-documentation. By typing in the word "help", you get a list of over 50 key words which you can use to get the specific kind of help you require. The system is oriented toward students who don't know much about computers and want to learn. Another bonus is an approximate 2/3 discount for connect time if you use the interactive system between 6:00 p.m. and 8:00 a.m. any night.

As you can see, the opportunities to use the Apple in conjunction with a time-sharing system are great. How the Apple will be used this way is only limited by the number of owners who try these additional capabilities of their table top marvel. I am aware of a realtor who is using his Apple for direct access to the real estate multiple listing service to which he subscribes. A couple of us are trying to get the Apple to store in its memory the data received from the large time-sharing systems. This will help us avoid the tedious chore of keying-in existing computerized data for manipulation in programs we have written for our Apples. I would really appreciate hearing from anyone who has already solved this problem.

TRANSIENT VOLTAGE PROTECTORS
By Steve Paulson

The transient voltages that we are concerned about are those which occur when any electric or electronic device is energized or de-energized. These interruptions in current flow cause "spikes" or peaks of voltage which are then transmitted to the computer. Since the computer uses very defined voltages and currents for it's memory, logic and timing functions, these sudden changes in voltage and current can do great harm.

The Transient Voltage Protector is a device that utilizes several varistors to detect any transient voltages and then disperse them to ground. Sometimes (as in the turning on of an electric range, refrigerator, light switch, or any number of electric devices), these transient voltages can be as high as 1200 volts and more. One might imagine the damage that could occur if these voltages were to enter the small silicon chips of the Apple.

The Transient Voltage Protector is a simple device that plugs into the wall outlet and then the computer (or any device) is then plugged into the protector. One should make sure the protector is rated at a sufficient level to provide protection. A rule-of-thumb is that it should be able to handle voltages of at least four times the source. That is, for the Apple, one would need protection of at least 500 volts.

KEY KLICKER ROUTINE

If you have a newer Apple with the silent keyboard, Don Williams has written a short and sweet machine language routine to solve your problem.

```
0300:   48          PHA
0301:   A9 20       LDA  #$20
0303:   8D 30 C0    STA  $C030
0306:   20 A8 FC    JSR  $FCA8
0309:   8D 30 C0    STA  $C030
030C:   68          PLA
030D:   4C 1B FD    JMP  $FD1B
0038:   00 03
```

Once you store the address ($0300) in location $38 and hit return, your keys will click merrily away until you hit reset. To restart the routine, reenter the address.

A minor modification of this routine will give you a slow list (with tones) feature. Change the JMP and 030D to F0FD and store the address in $36. The value stored at $0302 may be increased for a slower list.

```
Apple
Pugetsound
Program                           01.08.79
Library
Exchange
```

Memb. list	____
Mail. list	____
App. fee	____
Dues	____
Call -Apple	

A.P.P.L.E. is an Apple user group, not affiliated with Apple Computer, Inc., and provides the following member benefits: Monthly meetings on third Tuesday of each month; Call -Apple, a monthly newsletter with many programming hints, current news, etc.; "Apple hot line", a service to assist primarily newcomers to personal computing with answers to questions on hardware and software; last but not least, the Program Library, a collection of software available to members at little or no cost. Dues are composed of $2.50 Apple-Cation Fee and $7.50 annual dues.

MEMBERSHIP APPLE-CATION

1. Name_____ Date_____

2. Street Address_____

3. City_____ State, Zip_____

4. Phones (a) Home_____ (b) Work_____

5. System Description_____

6. Software background_____

7. Hardware background_____

8. Are you available to assist other members?_____

9. In what field?_____

10. In what area can the club assist you?_____

11. May we furnish your name/address/phone to others?_____

12. Special Interest group Information
         Examples: Ham Radio, Medical, Astrology

    _____

    _____

13. Total amount enclosed_____

14. What will you use your Apple II for?_____

    _____

15. Comments_____

    _____

    _____

Apple
Puget Sound
Program
Library
Exchange

COLLECTOR'S ITEM

The first edition
of CALL-A.P.P.L.E.

C/O Val J. Golding
6708 39th Ave. S.W.
Seattle, Wa. 98136
(206) 937-6588 (Home)
(206) 623-7966 (Work)

February 7, 1978

Dear Apple Owner:

The purpose of this letter is to form an Apple computer users group, as indicated by the tentative name above, and to further the exchange of information and programs of interest to Apple users.

A preliminary meeting has been set for 7 PM Thursday, Feb. 16th at Computerland, 1500 S. 336th St., Federal Way, Wa. 98003 (Phones 927-8585 and 838-9363).

Unfortunately, I do not have the time available to continue this project beyond the formative stage; therefore the first order of business will be (hopefully) to find someone that can. I see this group as a very useful organization and I will certainly be available for assistance.

The APPLE goals, as conceived, should include establishing a software library for exchanging programs on a cost-only basis, Programming assistance, the exchange of information on Apple-compatible equipment and periferals and the publication of a brief newsletter as a medium for some of the above items.

You are urged, therefore, to attend this meeting, and if for any reason you can not attend but are interested in this group, please contact me for further details as they develope.

PROGRAM EXCHANGE

The following programs are already available at no cost:
ZOT = A one way conversation with your computer.
STAR WARS= Galactic target practice using your paddles.
STOP WATCH= A real time clock and stop watch for your Apple.
HEX-DEC= A conversion program that converts Hex to Dec. and back.
ANNE APPLE= An interactive rap session with your computer.
        Bring tape and recorder with you

EQUIPMENT

DAK HEC-60 Casettes @ .73 each (good quality) See me to order.
APPLE IO Board from Electronics Warehouse $74 assembled.
IP-125 Hard copy printer by Integral data $799. See Feb. Byte.
"HOW TO PROGRAM MICROCOMPUTERS" Sams #21459 available from
Computerland and Retail Computer Store. A MUST at $8.95.

APPLE PUGETSOUND PROGRAM LIBRARY EXCHANGE

6708 39TH AVENUE SW   SEATTLE, WA. 98136

A.P.P.L.E. MEMBER PRICE AND DESCRIPTION LIST AS OF JANUARY 1, 1979 ALL PRICES POSTPAID

PROGRAMS ON CASSETTE

PROGRAMMER'S WORKSHOPINTEGER VERSION 9.13	$ 6.50	_____
PROGRAMMER'S WORKSHOPDISK VERSION 10.24	$ 6.50	_____
APPLESOFTWORKSHOP VERSION 1.0	$ 6.50	_____
WORKSHOP UPDATES	$ 2.50	_____
LIBRARY PAK 1B	$ 5.50	_____
LIBRARY PAK 2	$ 5.50	_____
LIBRARY PAK 3	$ 5.50	_____
LIBRARY PAK 4	$ 5.50	_____
INTEGER BASIC TUTORIAL PROGRAMS	$ 17.50	_____
6502 FORTH (PROGRAMMING LANGUAGE)	$ 35.00	
WORD PROCESSOR/TEXT EDITOR	AVAILABLE SOON	
APMAIL < REQUIRES DISK >	12.50	_____

PROGRAMS ON DISK

APMAIL	17.50	_____
DISK PAK 34 < LIBRARY PAK 3 & 4 >	15.00	_____
DISK PAK 12 < LIBRARY PAK 1B & 2 >	AVAILABLE SOON	
WORKSHOP DISK PAK (INTEGER & APPLESOFT	17.50	_____

OTHER ITEMS

BALANCE DUE OR CREDIT BALANCE	_____	_____
CALL -APPLE BACK ISSUES, 1979	$ 1.25	_____
PEEKING AT CALL -APPLE, VOL I, 1978	$ 7.50	_____
WOZPAK	$ 18.50	_____
MEMBERSHIP APPLE-CATION FEE	$ 2.50	_____
1979 A.P.P.L.E. DUES	$ 7.50	_____
PROGRAM SUBMISSION FORMS	S.A.S.E	_____
TOTAL AMOUNT ENCLOSED		_____

****

LIBRARY PAK 1B CONTAINS
SOFTCORE SOFTWARE, LIFE, STOPWATCH, ALPHABET
HIRES PAK I < BIORHYTHM & 3 OTHER DEMOS >
COLOR GAME PAK < 5 PROGRAMS >
COLOR DEMO PAK < SKETCH, WORM, 4 OTHERS >
CASINO GAME PAK < PINBALL, 21, ONE ARM BANDIT >
EDUCAT'L GAMEPAK < HAMMURABI, 2 OTHERS >
STAR WARS II, APPLEODIAN, ROCKET LANDER

LIBRARY PAK 2 CONTAINS
LIMITED CASETTE OPERATING SYSTEM
COLOR GAMEPAK I < KLINGON CAPTURE, 4 OTHERS >
COLOR GAMEPAK II < MARBLE DROP, 3 OTHERS >
COLOR GAMEPAK III <TOWER OF HANOI, 3 OTHERS >
COLOR DEMOPAK II < MAZE, BIT BIN, 2 OTHERS >
HOLIDAY GREETINGPAK < XMAS TREE, CAKE, 8 OTHERS >
BATTLESHIP, NIGHTMARE GAMEPAK <5 GAMES >

LIBRARY PAK 3 CONTAINS
MUSICPAK I <2 VOICE MUSIC, 2 OTHERS >
APPLEWARS, HAPPY BIRTHDAY
COLOR GAMEPAK IV < COUNTRY DRIVER +3 >
EDUCAT'L PAK II < SELL LEMONADE, ETC. >

LIBRARY PAK 4 CONTAINS
POET, SPIROLATERAL
PRINTER PAK I < CALENDAR, 2 OTHERS >
FINANCIAL PAK < AMORTIZATION, 17 OTHERS >
LORES SHAPES USING THE &

WORKSHOP CONTAINS
APPEND, RENUM, BYTES, EXAM, POKE
CATALOG, LIST, MONITOR, QUIT, ETC.
APPLESOFT VERSION REQUIRES ROM CARD

APMAIL CONTAINS
9 DATA FIELDS, WILL SEARCH OR
SORT ON ANY, OUTPUT ALL DATA,
OR LABELS TO PRINTER OR SCREEN

FILL OUT TOP HALF AND RETURN, ALONG WITH APPLE-CATION BLANK AND CHECK

APPLE II® LIGHT PEN

The PROGRAMMA Apple II Light Pen is an input peripheral device that can be connected to the Apple II Computer System without any modifications to the hardware. The Light Pen plugs directly into the Game I/O connector.

The PROGRAMMA Apple II Light Pen may be used in numerous applications which may require the user to select a choice from a menu that is being displayed. Some examples of menu selection are exhibited by the pictures in this advertisement.

Low resolution graphics are also a possible application of the PROGRAMMA Apple II Light Pen.

The PROGRAMMA Apple II Light Pen comes assembled and tested. Three sample demonstration programs are included which instruct the user on how to use the Light Pen in application programs. A User Operator's Manual is also included.

The PROGRAMMA Apple II Light Pen is available today from your Apple Computer Dealer. It is also available mail order through PROGRAMMA International, Inc., the professionals with quality Software and Hardware Computer Products.

PRICE: $34.95

Please include $2.00 Postage and handling. California residents add 6% sales tax.

Apple II is a registered trademark of Apple Computers, Inc.

VISA   MASTERCHARGE

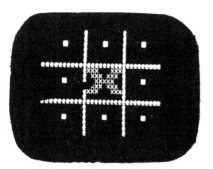

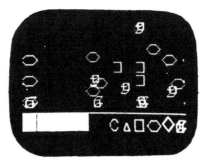

PROGRAMMA
INTERNATIONAL, Inc.
3400 Wilshire Blvd.
Los Angeles, CA 90010
(213) 384-0579

PROGRAMMA

Hardware
Products

DEALER INQUIRIES INVITED

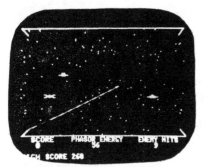
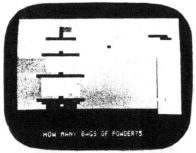
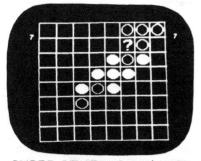

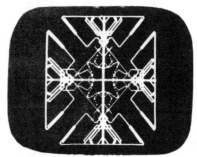

www.ingramcontent.com/pod-product-compliance
Lightning Source LLC
Chambersburg PA
CBHW082123070326
40690CB00049B/4202